THE
TEN
COMMANDMENTS

THE
TEN
COMMANDMENTS

Laws of the Heart

JOAN
CHITTISTER

ORBIS BOOKS
Maryknoll, New York 10545

Second Printing, March 2007

Founded in 1970, Orbis Books endeavors to publish works that enlighten the mind, nourish the spirit, and challenge the conscience. The publishing arm of the Maryknoll Fathers and Brothers, Orbis seeks to explore the global dimensions of the Christian faith and mission, to invite dialogue with diverse cultures and religious traditions, and to serve the cause of reconciliation and peace. The books published reflect the views of their authors and do not represent the official position of the Maryknoll Society. To learn more about Maryknoll and Orbis Books, please visit our website at www.maryknoll.org.

Manufactured in the United States of America

Library of Congress Cataloging-in-Publication Data

Chittister, Joan.
    The Ten commandments : laws of the heart / Joan Chittister.
      p. cm.
    ISBN-13: 978-1-57075-684-9
    1. Ten commandments. I. Title.
  BV4655.C515 2006
  241.5′2 – dc22

                                        2006010328

Contents

Contents

Introduction

We need to think again about the moral fibers of society. We need to think about them a great deal in fact. If we fail to rethink what it means to be a Christian, to be a carrier of the Judeo-Christian tradition, in this day and age, the next day and age may be far more stark, exceedingly more threatening, extremely less hopeful, seriously less spiritual than any we have ever known before.

We must rethink what it means to be a moral agent in this society.

We must begin to reconsider what it means to be a moral person, a holy person, in an age when small personal behaviors affect not only our own lives but the lives of people around the globe.

We are poised on the brink of a newly shaped world. If we make it. But for the first time in human history, the entire human race is strapped in tandem as we go. What we once called "progress" has turned against us, snapping at our heels.

John Reid, secretary of defense in England, for instance, in a high-level meeting of British political, scientific, and public figures, ranked climate changes due to global warming alongside international terrorism, demographic changes, and global energy demand as one of the major threats facing the world in future decades.

Within twenty to thirty years, Reid predicts, the world will not be fighting wars over oil. It will be fighting wars over water.

Tony Blair, England's prime minister, is holding "crisis Downing Street summits" in order to address the problem.

But what does that have to do with the average Christian today?

In the United States, we are still debating whether there is such a thing as global warming, despite overwhelming scientific evidence from around the globe.

Experts tell us, for instance, that people need fifty liters of water a day to live comfortably. Even twenty-five liters a day will cover basic human needs. But in Mozambique people have access to fewer than ten liters a day. In England, on the other hand, British citizens use an average of two hundred liters a day. In the United States, we use five hundred. Each. Every day. In the West, we use eight liters of water just to brush our teeth. We use between a hundred and two hundred liters to take a shower.

Is that moral or not?

What is sin?

What moral principles should we be steering by and how do we know?

The society is alive with the question and the tensions it brings with it. For instance, I have a friend who writes to me regularly about the deplorable state of religion in the United States. He wants prayer in public schools. "Whose prayer?" I write back. The letters stop for awhile.

Then it gets to be Christmas and he wants a crib set on the grounds of the local courthouse. "What about the menorah for Hanukkah?" I ask. He's not so sure about that. "Well, Santa Claus is there," I point out. He ignores the remark and ends the conversation.

After a while, he hears that Bible study is being challenged in public schools. He's incensed. "How would you feel about being required to study world religions?" I press. He goes away fuming.

Later, after two Supreme Court cases that contest the use of religious figures in government buildings, the letters start again. He can't imagine a civil system that is not based on the Judeo-Christian Ten Commandments. He is especially committed to the notion that a display of the Sinai Tablets should hang in local courtrooms. "What about the Koran and its shariah law? Or the Lotus Sermons and the Buddhist Precepts? Or the Bhagavad-Gita and the Vedas?" I wonder. "After all," I point out, "there are over 1 million Hindus and 1.5 million Buddhists in the United States — and the numbers are growing." He's quiet for a time, but he'll be back with more demands for religious purity, more concerns about the loss of Christian principles in a secular world. And soon. After all, on those issues, he says, rests the future of this country, all other religious systems here notwithstanding.

The questions he raises are real ones. They are not to be ignored, nor taken lightly, nor ridiculed, nor dismissed as meaningless.

What's most important about the conversations, perhaps, is that this friend of mine is not alone in his consternation.

The man is not unusual. He's no zealot, no fanatic, no evangelist. On the contrary, he's a good, hardworking, sensible, mainstream American — and, if the social science data is correct, a more typical one than not. He simply demonstrates what has been a longstanding mark of U.S. history: religion is not a matter of indifference in this country. On the contrary. Continuing attendance at public worship of some sort makes the United States of America one of the most churchgoing nations in the world.

But as much as there is continuing commitment to the Judeo-Christian tradition that is embodied in the Ten Commandments, there is also a growing confusion about exactly what they now mean. When the chief financial officers of a major corporation are charged with fraud of stockholders or overpricing of consumers, is that really stealing or just smart business practices?

How did all that swearing get to be so commonly accepted in a country that calls itself "religious"? Is it blasphemy?

We are awash in the struggle to resolve the moral dimensions of the abortion problem in Christianity but not at all exercised about the wanton killing of civilians — now the major casualties of modern conflict — in warfare.

More than the private practice of religion, however, the public or social dimension of religious commitment is just as significant here. "Religion," Americans say in survey after survey, "has an important role to play in contemporary society." We do not, in this country, believe in hiding who we are or what we believe or why we do what we do as a nation — and how whatever it is almost surely comes out of our different religious beliefs.

Unlike political candidates in most other countries of the world who make no reference to their religious affiliations whatsoever, presidential candidates in this country make it a point to be seen going to church. In fact, political candidates in this country ignore to their peril the religious sensitivities of religious lobbies. The "religious" vote has affected one election after another from Al Smith, the first Catholic candidate for president, to George W. Bush, right-leaning Evangelical.

The history of religion in the United States, in fact, has always been a volatile one. However constant the myth of religious freedom and religious tolerance in the country — and maybe even because of it — religion is a very public subject here. Perhaps never more so than now.

Thousands of people who sailed the Atlantic Ocean to settle this country came for religious reasons: refuge, freedom, experimentation. They came to be religious in new ways and old, yes — as Protestants, Quakers, Old Believers, Catholics — but at the same time they came sharing a common religious worldview. They came to live the Judeo-Christian ethic, the Ten Commandments, better, more authentically, more fully here than they felt had been possible for them in the lands from which they came.

But what did that mean?

What has it ever meant?

What are the Ten Commandments and what do they mean to us now in a world where Jew, Christian, and Muslim all claim to embrace Moses and the Tablets of Sinai as the foundation of our law, however many other laws we all add to them?

This book takes these questions seriously. It is not a checklist of "sins" — like in periods past. It is, instead, an attempt to look at what we have traditionally seen as the foundation of our society, as well as the core of our own moral behavior, from three perspectives, to lift each of them up and look at it from multiple perspectives, to consider again what it means on both a personal and a social level.

This book intends to look again at both the historical background and the present implications of the Ten Commandments.

Each of the commandments is presented from three different points of view. First, I look at the historical understanding of the commandment. I examine what it meant in the context of the early Jewish community itself. Then I look at situations to which the commandment applies today. Finally, I present reflection statements for personal consideration that are designed to broaden our personal perspective and provoke thought about what it really means to follow those commandments and live by their principles in our own time.

If we are really a people steeped in the Ten Commandments — culturally, politically, socially — and intent on preserving them as the bedrock of our own civilization, what does that mean for us, here and now? Are the life principles they provide for us truly living impulses in us or simply a relic of past ages that has become a kind of cultural fetish, something that distinguishes us from the religious world around us, perhaps, but that is of little actual consequence in either our personal or public lives.

Is there anything in them to really care about, or are they simply artifacts of another world? Are they really any kind of criterion for our own lives? What do they measure in us? And who cares?

The Ten Commandments of the Hebrew people were not a unique element of their society or the era in which they lived. Every culture of the ancient Middle East had laws. The Code of Hammurabi, for instance, one of the most famous of all early law codes, both stabilized and promulgated the standards by which the king intended to order society. Until Hammurabi, law was essentially the whim of the king. Laws were created at the fancy of the king, and they could be changed by him at any moment.

Hammurabi, king of Babylon, made a giant leap forward in the history of public jurisprudence. He bound himself and the citizenry to 272 statutes, which he had inscribed on a pillar more than fourteen feet high for all his kingdom to see. The Code of Hammurabi brought order and stability to the land. For the first time, royal decree ceased to be arbitrary. For the first time, people were allowed to know the laws under which they would be governed and judged.

At least four hundred years later, Moses, who had led the Hebrew people out of slavery in Egypt, gave the little band of wanderers another set of "laws" to live by. These laws, however, embodied the mind of God for them; they carved them into a society unique for its adherence not to the laws of Moses — subject to change by any ruler to follow — but to the law of God. They did not emerge out of human whim and fancy. They were irrevocable and unchangeable. They were to be written on the mind and in the heart of the Hebrew community for all time to come.

The giving of the Ten Commandments can be seen instantly to be unique. These laws were meant to be more principles to live by than minutely defined proscriptions to be followed. These laws were clearly meant to shape a way of living, a lifestyle, an attitude of mind, a spirit of human community, a people.

The Ten Commandments of the Hebrew people were more than simple ordinances and their corresponding punishments, important as these emerging codes would become to the achievement of public peace and order.

The Ten Commandments were not made to be argued in a court of law. In fact, most of the items defined in the Ten Commandments were not legally enforceable at all. Many of them could not even be discovered, in fact. How did anyone prosecute for "coveting"? How did anyone punish someone for not "remembering" to keep holy the Sabbath? How could anyone tell if, in the heart of a person, a "strange" God or two might not be lurking?

The fact is that the public self and the private self are often a counterweight to one another. The tension between the two, in fact, is the very definition of the spiritual life. Each calls the other to growth. Or to put it another way, I can't begin to count how often I've heard, "I'm a Catholic, but I don't believe that birth control is wrong." Both statements are true. Which one will grow into the other, no one knows. But one thing we can be sure of is that each of them has something to do with the ideal for which our lives seek.

The point is that the Ten Commandments are laws of the heart, not laws of the commonwealth. They are laws that are intended to lead to the fullness of life, not simply to the well-ordered life.

Aristotle insists that the perfect life is one where we contemplate the best, most worthy things, the things of highest merit. The perfect life, he argues, commits us to dedicate ourselves to what it is that is worth thinking about. The Ten Commandments tell us what's worth thinking about in life.

These are the things beyond the culture, above the culture, more important than the transitory mechanics of the daily. These are the things that perdure, that become the spiritual ground on which our lives rest, that become the path we walk on the journey to wholeness from the smallest to the most expansive of human endeavors.

These are not so much new laws as they are a new vision of what it is to be a human community, a people of God. Moses, scripture points out, is required to delay the promulgation of the law until the Hebrew people are finally in the Promised Land, until they are finally ready to settle down and begin a whole new way of living.

Most significant of all, perhaps, is that only once in scripture, in Exodus 34, are the Sinai Tablets called "commandments" at all. The truth is that they are not actually statutes because they indicate no punishment for disobeying them.

Instead, in all the other references to Sinai in scripture, the Ten Commandments are referred to as the Decalogue — "the ten words." It is the Decalogue, these ten words that over the years developed into ten ideas or concepts or ideals or propositions, that make the twelve tribes of Israel a different kind of "people." They are words about praise, human responsibility, justice, creation, the value of life, the nature of relationships, honesty, veracity, desire, and simplicity of life.

Written in second person singular, "You shall" and "You shall not," the "words" are meant to be a whole new way of going about life for us all. We have been told this time, not what the king expects, but what God expects — and we are each responsible for sculpting our lives in that mold.

The Ten Commandments are, then, an adventure in human growth. We are not so much convicted by them as we are to be transformed by them.

In the end, the transformation is so much more important than the sport of public display. All the Christmas cribs on courtyard lawns in the world will not make us a people of the Decalogue. In fact, it can be argued that the Ten Commandments themselves — with their warnings about false gods and graven images — are very cautious about such things. All the Sinai Tablets on the walls of all the courtrooms in the land will not assure us of justice in the courts if we do not have hearts already shaped by what the sculptures signify. All the prayers and prayer meetings in the world that we hold in public schools in a pluralistic society will not make us people of the law unless the law lives first in our hearts. And if it does, the displays will not much matter. We ourselves will be their sign.

First

THE LAW OF REFLECTION

I, the Lord, am your God, you shall not have other gods besides me. — Exodus 20:3

In the beginning . . .

The little girl didn't know a lot, but she knew what she knew. She also knew that learning things had something do with growing up. "Remember now," the nun aunt called from the doorway. "Don't get too close to the edge of the pool." The little girl looked up quietly, and the nun disappeared from the doorway.

"Don't run on the tile," the nun called out through the family room window a few minutes later. "You might fall and get hurt." The little girl frowned a bit and turned her head away.

"Be careful, Caroline," the nun called again. "You don't want to fall in the pool."

The little girl stood up exasperated. "Aunt Alice," she said, hands on her hips. "I'm six!"

13

The story is clear: We aren't born fully mature adults. But we do grow. Every stage of life teaches us something. Every experience adds to the depth of our insight. Every situation requires something new of us. At every juncture we are deeper, wiser people.

Like all of us, the Hebrew people grew over the centuries in their understanding, both of themselves and of God. Over time, "the ten words" begin to be enlarged, developed, defined, explained.

The process of moral development of this people is easily traced. By comparing the law as it exists in the earlier book of the covenant with the law as it is stated later in Deuteronomy, we begin to see the subtle changes that marked a growing sense of conscience. In its earliest version, for instance, Hebrew law about the release of slaves applies only to male slaves. Later, in Deuteronomy, however, the law applies equally to both male and female slaves. In the later law, too, not only must slaves be emancipated every seventh year, but they are not to be sent off penniless. They must be provided for — and their wives and children as well.

The same kind of growth, scholars tell us, applies to the development of the Decalogue itself. Israel always recognized Yahweh as the greatest of the gods, for instance, but the notion that there was only one God grows only slowly in Hebrew consciousness.

Scripture leaves us no doubt about the situation. Rachel steals the household gods of her father, Laban, as she and Jacob return to his land. Samuel, under siege, fears that he will be sent "to serve other gods" in a foreign land. Israel adopts a pantheon of gods, of which the psalmist sings that Yahweh is supreme but not unique. Psalm 82 begins: "God has taken his place in the divine council; in the midst of the gods he holds judgment." Solomon, one of Israel's greatest kings, built a great temple to Yahweh, true, but Solomon built temples to other gods, as well (1 Kings 11:3).

Not until six hundred years after Moses does Israel, through the prodding of the prophets, even begin to define for itself the meaning and implications of theoretical monotheism.

It's a comforting thought.

The truth is that we all grow into the spiritual life. Slowly.

All of us have more than one god, if only we could ever admit it. It can take a lifetime to understand that all life can only come from one source, that we have frittered away a great part of ours on lesser idols, that we have worshiped at chimerical shrines of our own making.

The power of the commandment lies in the fact that it calls us back to remember what is really ultimate, really important in life. It sets out to save us from the delusions we serve that, in the end, never fail to disappoint us. We put our hope in the power of money and find that when we get it nothing changes. We go from one relationship to another and find out that we are still not able to deal with them well. We are no more able to find love than when we first thought we had it and even less sure of the loves we do have now. We find deference but not respect.

We see the power of social connections to give us what we do not have within us and discover, if we're lucky, that all we will ever really have is whatever it is inside us that we have cultivated ourselves. When other people are our self-confidence, our spiritual gurus, our definition of self, our self-esteem, our courage, and our truth, we are only pretending to be alive.

When we satiate the senses in order to avoid the taste of life in all its raw and unmarinated potential, when we make sensual satisfactions — drugs and alcohol, sex and physical comfort — our gods in order to damp the pain of living, we only live the shell of a life.

Then we surround ourselves with idols that block our vision of what it means to know the self, to grow, to see the glory of God in the most inglorious of places.

It is so easy to criticize the gods of the other, to practice a kind of ecclesiastical imperialism and think ourselves faithful to the first commandment. But that is light years away from an understanding of the God of All. In that one God is the cry for oneness in us.

To condemn as faithless, as pagan, those whose own sense of God is other than ours is to deny the process of creation itself. Human creatures are born in a day and then take years to become the persons they are meant to be. The spiritual life is a slowly dawning process. It happens in the same way that the human becomes fully conscious — not all at once, the neurologists tell us, but more like the turning up of a dimmer switch. In the course of that time, we have a great deal to learn about God from those who call God by another name, too, who define God in other words, who worship God in different tones and rhythms.

For the sake of the God in which we say we believe, we do very ungodlike things to people whose color is different than ours, whose language is different than ours, whose gender is different than ours. We make our nations, our race, and our sex God and in the doing of it, make our religions irreligious and our God puny.

We do our idol worship in the name of God. We make God in our own image — and that is the most pitiable idol of them all. It makes us our own God and our national, global, ecclesiastical decisions show it. With only ourselves at the center of our lives, we lose a sense of the eternal, the global, the cosmic. We miss the vision of the whole. We struggle against the wrong demons. We worship at the most evanescent of shrines.

And so one national power supersedes another and we all suffer from the delusions of delusion as a result. We wander blindly through life and never even know we're blind. We hear no one but ourselves and fail to recognize the impairment. We arrest the journey of the soul to greatness in midflight and never even realize the paresis. We think we are on our way to somewhere and have not a notion that we walking a treadmill to nowhere.

Like the concept of monotheism, the Hebrew rejection of idol worship was long in coming. But with it came the notion of the otherness of God. If God could not be contained in material images, God was more than matter, above matter, beyond matter.

Our God, it is clear, is not of human making, not of this world, not to be reduced to anything material. Not surprisingly, then, early Christianity, too, refused to use images. Even representations of the crucified body of Jesus are not found before the sixth century, when the need to educate the masses made images the books of the illiterate.

But now, like the early Israelites, we make our graven images for years before we come to realize, if we ever do, that the image is powerless to save. Image-making, after all, is what the modern world does best. If we look the part, we assume we are the part: we buy the right clothes, drive the right cars, drink the right drinks, and think we become the hero, the mogul, the beautiful one, the star, the powerful one whose trappings we imitate. We take on the images and play the parts and live in the shadows of those who do it best and fool ourselves into thinking that we have become the thing, the god we have come to adore. Madison Avenue, that great image machine of the Western world, assures us that we have. And we are inclined to believe it.

That's when the first commandment becomes so important.

The first commandment prods us to examine again and again what it is that we have put before God in our lives, what it is we have made our gods instead.

Then we come to understand that it is this commandment that is meant to keep us in touch with the verities of life, that gives us balance, that gives us hope that, despite our own slowness, God is there at the end of the journey, waiting, supporting us in the struggle to grow up spiritually, bringing us home.

And then...

When I was growing up, they gave us tiny little stitched pamphlets to help us prepare for confession. The book had ten chapters. In it, each of the Ten Commandments was followed by a list of behaviors said to be more or less sinful. Every Saturday afternoon I knelt in the back of church pouring over the thing, trying to figure out my sins.

"Mortal" sins, the ones that endangered your immortal soul, they printed in CAPITAL LETTERS. "Venial" sins, sins that showed a serious predilection for unsavory behavior but not enough, ordinarily, to be of major consequence, like murder or missing Mass, they printed in lower case. The little book was meant to help small kids know what to say to the priest in the confessional.

The first commandment, they told us, was "I am the Lord your God. You shall not have strange gods before me." I spent years trying to figure out what you would have to do to break this one.

After all, God was God. How could you deny that? I had never even seen a fortune-teller, let alone go to one. And I certainly never prayed to anybody named either Baal or Beelzebub. So, truth is, this chapter I skipped.

Now I'm older and I figure that I spent far too little time on the first commandment; far too much time on a few of the other ones. The truth is that this commandment may be the easiest one of them all to break.

It may also be the one that does us the most harm of all of them, not so much to other people but to ourselves.

Once you start letting this one slip by, life takes on a very purple hue.

This is the commandment that decides the orientation of our whole lives. This one asks us who or what we are making God now.

This is the one that decides where we're likely to get stuck in life. This is the one that determines where we'll turn when things get tough.

The first commandment is the commandment that is meant to lead us home, not only to our God but to ourselves.

And for you ...

Love of things leads us from one blessing to another in life. Clinging to things that cannot last only leads us from one pain to another in life. Only God lasts.

We have no scientific proof that there is a God and we have no scientific proof that there is not a God. All we have is the low, clear voice within saying always, "There must be more to this than this." And that is all the proof we need.

Hindus name 330 million gods in a metaphorical attempt to make the point that no amount of imagination can capture the One Who Is.

The tendency to define absolute truth, as if we ourselves were God and could do it, smacks of idol worship, too. Only this time we make ourselves the false god we adore.

The Koran teaches, "God is the East and the West, and wherever you turn, there is God's face." If only we could see beyond what of God is in ourselves, we could begin to see the wonders of God around us and in the rest of the religions of the world as well.

The shortest distance to God is not an excursion through all the experiences of life. It is the journey we take to the center of the self where God waits for us within.

21

Whatever it is that you give your life to is the shrine at which you adore. The question is, Is this a big enough god for anyone to spend a life on?

God is always just beyond what we think is god. That's why we must continue to look beyond everything that now captivates us for what it is meant to model.

"God will be present," a Latin proverb teaches, "whether asked or not." God does not "find" me. God is with me already. It is a matter of my becoming conscious of the God who has already found me.

My entry into God is always an unexpected one. Sometimes it is joy; sometimes pain. Sometimes it is beauty; sometimes horror. The important thing to remember is that it is always at the deepest point of my soul. "God," Emerson says, "enters by a private door into every individual."

God is an experience, not a thing and not an idea. The moment you determine that you have found God, beware which god it is. If it is the God of rules and thought, doubt it. Blaise Pascal says, "It is the heart that experiences God, and not reason."

As long as God is "he," that God is a false God. If God is pure spirit, God is neither male nor female. In the words of theologian Sandra Schneiders, "No matter how entrenched in the imagination of the average Christian the image of a male God might be, theological tradition has never assigned sex to God." Strange, isn't it, how even religion can create its own false gods?

Second

THE LAW OF RESPECT

You shall not take the name of the Lord, your God, in vain. — Exodus 20:7

In the beginning...

The 2005 Lutheran Convention, at a moment of great dissension over the acceptance of homosexual ministers in the denomination, voted first 851–127 that they would remain united, whatever the outcome of the vote on the admission of gays to ordained Lutheran ministry. "Our job is not to judge one another; our job is to love one another," said Patrick Monroe of the Central/Southern Illinois Synod, speaking in favor of unity. "This motion allows us to move forward in that way, not just with sexual issues but with all issues."

That may be one of the finest displays of commitment to the second commandment that the church will ever have. This was a group of Christians who did not use God to curse to hell those among them who differed from them in their joint attempt to interpret the will of God for the church in a new age facing new questions. This was a church in process, in pilgrimage, that did not pretend that any of them knew the full mind of God for all time. This was a body of Christians who did not use God against one another in a display of arrogance known for its unflinching certitude.

In every adult heart lingers the fragments of a child's nursery rhyme. Learned at an early age, it was designed to make us all invulnerable to criticism, derision, and rejection. "Sticks and stones," they taught us to chant, "can break my bones, but names will never hurt me." But, if truth were told, the rhyme indicated a major change in human consciousness.

For centuries, the world knew that such bravado was patently wrong. Names could hurt us. What we called a thing had serious implications. To invoke the name of the gods, for instance, was to call down a spirit — a power far greater than anything humans could muster of themselves. To show deference, respect, awe, the Hebrew people never even used the name of God.

When Moses asks God at the burning bush, then, "What is your name? Who will I say sent me?" it is no idle question. He is looking for credentials that will not only justify his going to pharaoh but provide him with the resources, the protection, the support he will need to do it. The question does not mean to him and the Hebrew people what we mean when we shake hands and say to a stranger, "And you are...?" To Moses, the name itself would be a sign of the authenticity of the message, the sanctity of his call, the power of his position.

To all ancient peoples, names had meaning, names had power. According to the linguist, S. Potter, "A primitive man felt that the relationship between name and thing...was close and intimate. The frivolous or malicious handling of a name in speech might imply insult or injury to the person bearing that name. The very name was hallowed."

In every ancient culture, naming — knowing the essence of the thing — was part of a person's identity. More than that, it was some kind of signal of their place in life, their purpose, their role in the community, their power.

To name something — someone — was to endow them with the characteristics implied by the name itself.

Native Americans, for instance, named their children for the animal spirit they saw in them: Little Running Bear, Great Eagle Wing, Brave Wolf Hunter.

Even in modern societies, there remains to this day at least a remnant of that same philosophy. John D. Rockefeller III is not just the man down the street. In that name is embedded a history, a social standing, an origin, an expectation.

Indeed, when Moses asks God, "What is your name?" the question is charged with meaning.

And so is the answer. God answers, "My name is *'e'yeh aser e'yeh.'* I am who am." I am Being. I am Life. I am Creator. No wonder there is a commandment about taking God's name "in vain." To insult the Creator of the universe must be high-level moral madness.

Important as it is to realize how momentous the idea of insulting the God of Gods must surely be in an early culture, however, it is even more important to look again at how that might be happening in our own time. By us. After all, naming no longer has the sense of the magical in this culture that it has had in times past or cultures unlike our own. In fact, it has even greater meaning now.

At first glance, the second commandment does not seem to have much to do with us at all. Except maybe for a few curses here and there, most of those not serious.

At another level, however, the second commandment begins to expose a predilection for a different standard of divine-human relationships altogether.

Philo of Alexandria, a prominent intellectual of first-century Judaism, led a delegation to Rome in about 40 C.E. to argue on behalf of Jews who refused to participate in Roman emperor worship. Just because Jews would not participate in emperor worship, he contended, did not make them immoral or irreligious people. On the contrary. The Ten Commandments of Moses, he claimed, represented the best moral guide in all of humankind.

The Ten Commandments proved, Philo insisted, that Jews lived according to all the virtues known to the Greek philosophers, especially temperance, prudence, courage, and justice. What's more, he said, the Decalogue actually surpassed the Greek model in judgment, righteousness, and loving-kindness. These were, then, a people who, despite their refusal to participate in Roman worship of the gods, were nevertheless a very moral, a very spiritual community.

Philo's schema of values, when brought to bear on the second commandment even now, may come closest to revealing what we have too long forgotten about this second word of wisdom, this second call to be a different kind of people. The second commandment makes eminent good sense.

As Philo points out, the second commandment warns us against bringing God to bear witness to what should need no witness at all. Why, he argues, "swear" to anything at all? If we are telling the truth, swearing isn't necessary. And if we are lying, swearing it is true only makes the lie worse. Most serious of all, why dishonor the name of God — all being and so all truth — by calling on Divine Truth to bear witness to a lie?

It is a compelling argument: to swear to anything either brings our own integrity into question or risks insulting the integrity of God. It doesn't make truth any truer and it only risks making the effects of untruth worse. The situation is a weighty one.

But there is more to be considered here — judgment, righteousness, and loving-kindness — that has something to do with the way we live this commandment. And this may be where we all fall far more short than we might much think.

In fact, the second commandment — "You shall not take the name of the Lord, your God, in vain" — may be more the sin of the pious than the sin of the sinner.

The second commandment tells us not only not to risk the corruption of God's name; it also tells us not to play God with God's name, with God's being, with God's power. It tells us not to use God's name uselessly. It is useless to use God's name to prove the untrue. It is useless, as well, to use God's name to do what God would never do.

This is the sin of those who put themselves in the place of God.

These people assume that they know the mind of God and they judge the world around them by its standards — which they make up as they go. It's a "God-will-get-you-for-that" threat that no human has the knowledge or the right to make. It is heavy on fear and guilt. And it starts early: "God doesn't like little girls who...," we're taught. "God punishes little boys that...," we hear. So there's really not much use trying after that, is there? It is one thing to displease a parent, a teacher, a minister, even a constitution. But to displease God puts the whole discussion into another category entirely. Someone somewhere has decided that we are guilty of something and we will be damned — and so they do it.

Oh, yes, we have learned to take God's name "in vain" quite well.

We use God's name to prove our piety. We quote scripture at people and expect that the discussion is over, that when we have spoken, God has spoken.

We use God's name to manipulate God. We ask God to be on our side, to do our will, to harm the people we ourselves would like to harm. "Dear God, punish these people for their sins so the world will know how great you are." We prayed for years and years for the "conversion of Russia" but never our own.

We use God's name to avoid facing our own inadequacies. We ask God to do for us what we ought to be doing for ourselves — eliminating nuclear weapons, feeding the starving, paying decent wages and benefits, stopping war.

We use God's name to exert power over others. We threaten them with hell. We name them "bad" and "incorrigible" — and they become bad and incorrigible. We use God as a kind of club over groups and people and ideas of which we disapprove.

Finally, we use God's name to satisfy ourselves of our own piety and righteousness, all the while avoiding the hard questions of life around us. We pray our prayers requiring God to "hear the cries of the poor" and tell ourselves that we have done enough. Enough for the poor. Enough for the outcast.

Indeed, we have learned to "take God's name in vain" with great facility.

It may be time to rethink this entire commandment.

And then...

In my family, language was an exercise in imagination. My mother had a salty Irish turn of phrase that nailed whatever she thought to the wall. My father was a quiet man who never talked much under any circumstances but who "damned this" and "damned that" with alarming regularity.

She could excoriate the entire world in one well-frozen sentence. She brooked no subterfuge. He, on the other hand, never really excoriated much of anyone though he sounded fierce.

She unmasked every idea for what it was worth. He was gentle and accepting of just about everybody and confronted little or nothing. If what the church told me about the Ten Commandments was true, they told me little about her and plenty about him: according to the Ten Commandments as I knew them, he was clearly not going to go to heaven. He was forever taking "the Lord's name in vain." She never did.

But I see things differently now.

I see that we concentrated on "the Lord's name" and ignored "in vain" entirely. As a result, we may have missed the point of the commandment entirely: it's not so much using God's name that is wrong as it is that we invoke the name of God to justify ungodly things. There are simply some things we say about God that are useless, fruitless, futile, ineffectual, and worthless. To attribute things to God that God has nothing to do with is to make a mockery of God. And mockery has all the earmarks of sin, however you say it.

Those who invoke God to justify prejudice — to tell us who God accepts and who God doesn't; to explain oppression — to say that God wills servitude for some kinds of people but not for others; to enthrone absolutism — to say that this country, these rules, this institution is the only one beloved of God; to enshrine authoritarianism — to argue that there are some people who can never be questioned, speak about God "in vain." God made us all and loves us all. God works in many ways with people, not just one. God wants all of us to use our minds to be responsible for our own beliefs, not to rest our fate on following the insights, decisions, and dictates of others.

To take God's name in vain — to make God responsible for who we hate and who we hurt and how we cease to think and who becomes our god and conscience — is to make God the doer of our evil.

The Jews decided not to risk it. They never use the name of God at all. It might be a good idea.

The God of Abraham, in a world full of hexes, of curses, was a God who did not hex. This God was not a god who watched and waited to dangle human beings on the head of a pin or to sacrifice one people at the expense of another. When we use God for those purposes we have taken God's name "in vain."

The Sufi tell the story of the teacher who sent his disciples to have a new shirt made for the upcoming feast day. "This is a very busy time and so the shirt is still in process. But come back in a week," the tailor said, "and God willing, your shirt will be ready." But it was not. "Come back next week," the tailor said the second time, "and if God shines on us, your new shirt will be finished." But it was not. "Come back again tomorrow," the tailor said, "and if God blesses us, your new shirt will be waiting for you." When the disciples explained to their master the tale of the unfinished shirt, the master said, "Go back to the tailor and ask him how long it will take to finish the shirt if he leaves God out of it."

The second commandment tells us to leave God out of it when God has nothing to do with whether we do what we ought to or not. Anything else profanes the name of God. Corrupts it morally. Violates its sacred character. Links it with things unworthy of it.

And for you . . .

"Language is the light of the mind," John Stuart Mill wrote. But if that is true, then everything we say about

God either makes God greater or smaller than we are. What we really think about God shows in the way we speak.

What we call a thing determines the way people see it. A person is "fat" or "stocky," "upset" or "hysterical" depending on our point of view. Unfortunately, we do the same to God. We speak of God as an instrument of punishment — "God damn it," we say — or a source of blessing — "God bless you," we say, when what we are really doing is simply describing our own feelings and calling on God — in vain — to confirm our limited human views.

As Samuel Butler put it, " 'The Rhyme of the Ancient Mariner' would not have taken so well if it had been called 'The Old Sailor.' " Language gives a thing its value. It enables us to see and makes us blind at the same time. To talk about God as if God exists to do our small and angry biddings is to make a god no real God would ever be.

When we use the name of God to demean or diminish any other human being, it is not they whose merits we measure. It is ourselves. And in public. How embarrassing.

It isn't swearing that makes us bad. It's meaning ill when we do it that makes the difference.

Almost every major act of destruction in history has been done while calling on the name of God for its legitimation: the Crusades, the witch burnings, apartheid. And no one said a word about sinning against the second commandment. Which only proves how easy it is to become your own god.

We curse and swear in order to show how angry or how powerful we are. The problem is that it doesn't work. All we really show is how out of control we are.

"Language," Sheila Rowbotham wrote, "is one of the instruments of domination." When we berate the other in the name of God, we assume unto ourselves the power of God. And nothing can be farther from the truth. After all, how many things have you ever cursed that ever changed?

To preach that women or blacks, for instance, are not supposed to be equal to white men because, "God made it that way" is to take God's name "in vain." To justify the evil we do by blaming it on God is surely an evil in itself.

"When the sacred texts contradict the search for peace and justice," dharma master Cheng Yen explained to a group of government officials, "the sacred texts must be reinterpreted." That's the Chinese version of not taking God's name in vain.

God is not my own private, mobile hex sign meant to be used against anyone I don't like. God is what calls me to be godly.

"When you have spoken the word," an Arab proverb teaches, "it reigns over us. When it is unspoken, you reign over it." Wild expressions may be simply a form of innocent emotional release but emotional control is still better.

Third

THE LAW OF REMEMBRANCE

Remember to keep holy the Sabbath day.
— Exodus 20:8

In the beginning…

In my Grandmother Chittister's house, good Protestant that she was, absolutely nothing happened on Sunday except church, Sunday school, and the family meal. She did not play the radio. She did not sew. She did not work around the house.

You didn't have to be a philosopher in that house to figure out that Sunday was a different kind of day.

Grandma sang hymns to herself as she went from room to room throughout the day. She frowned if Grandpa hammered boards in the garage. She frowned at loud laughing. She frowned at anything "frivolous." She frowned at the very thought of doing anything secular. Going to a movie, playing games in the yard, having a party — shopping! — were entirely out of the question.

I didn't much like to be in Grandma Chittister's house on Sundays. It was so different from the rest of the week. It was so compelling. But, from her, I got a message about life that stayed with me forever. Life, I learned young, is about more than noise. Life is about listening to the music of the soul. Work is important but it can be a distraction from meaning. Reflection is of the essence of being human.

It has been a worthy lesson, indeed. But where did it come from? Why do we do it?

Perhaps the most impacting historical dimension of the origin of the Sabbath is that there isn't any. Try as they might, scholars simply cannot account, other than through what Georg Fohrer calls the "fertile fantasy of exegetes," for the certain origin of a regular, unremitting, universal celebration of Sabbath in the Hebrew community.

"Many attempts have been made," Dr. Ernst Kutsch writes, "to derive the Sabbath from non-Israelite practices ... but none of them have been shown to be certain. It was a day of Saturn, some say, borrowed from a tribe of smiths whose forges needed to be cooled down regularly. Others suggests that it was the day of the full moon ... although there is no evidence that this was a day of rest. A few suggest that it was analogous to the days marking the phases of the moon but that theory is least plausible of all since those days, unlike the

Sabbath, were considered 'evil' days. One suggests that it was a market day. The problem with that idea is that on the Sabbath, on the contrary, trade was specifically forbidden."

One thing for sure, whatever accounts for the institutionalization of Sabbath in Israel, it stands alone, as a result, among all the cultures of the ancient world in its tribute to the dignity of humanity. Sabbath, after all, is not about rest as in "retirement." Sabbath is about time and who gets it, about who gets it and how they use it.

On the Sabbath, life changed. The privileges and expectations of standard roles and relationships ceased. The world, as it operated from the end of one Sabbath to the beginning of another, halted, stopped in midair, suspended itself over time.

The Jewish concept of Sabbath, it seems, was unique. What's even more impacting is that it was not only a philosophy of life; it was a precept, a principle, a teaching. It was a wisdom word, a guide to the good life. A reminder to us that we are all "made in the image of God," human beings, equals.

Sabbath is the word that demands justice for every living thing.

But in this new world, Sabbath means less and less every day.

Sabbath, it is clear, comes out of Hebrew respect for the sacredness of all life and the grounds of human dignity. Sabbath is not a day of "rest" because people are tired. It is a day of rest because people are human and ought not to be driven to death, because every living thing requires time to renew itself, if not physically, certainly spiritually; if not spiritually, at least physically.

It is a day of protest against the enslavement of peoples anywhere. It is a day of reflection on the life that makes humanity more than simply an exercise in survival. Sabbath says that we must take the time to remember that we came from God and to determine what we are doing daily in the process of returning there.

"You have made us little less than the angels," the psalmist sings — and the whole Sabbath world sings it with them.

Sabbath confronted two ideas in the ancient world: first, the common understanding that leisure was a privilege only of the gods; second, that humans were slaves to be used for the sake of the few free men who owned them. The Hebrew Sabbath gave — required — rest for everyone, slave and free, human and animal alike. The Hebrew Sabbath made equals of us all. It is an ancient, unique, and even startling view of the nature of life, the dignity of the human race.

Unfortunately, we stand on the brink of losing the concept again. Only this time, we have enslaved ourselves as well as failed to notice the new kinds of slavery that are being created around us.

People on fixed incomes fear for their old age as they see retirement about to slip away from them.

The poor go on working for a minimum wage of $5.15 an hour that makes any kind of rest impossible for them.

Working-class people are forced to work two part-time jobs if they cannot simply find one full-time job because part-time jobs provide no benefits.

Children in developing countries are being forced to work seventy-hour work weeks to provide consumer products for the Western world.

Animals, rather than being cared for, are wantonly destroyed in order to provide humans with cosmetics and jewelry and coats.

Sabbath cries out for resolution now before we all forget what it is trying to say to us in the midst of the consuming commercialism, the narcissistic exploitation of the goods of the earth and international chaos that now wracks the globe.

Sabbath says that we have forgotten who we are — that we are humans, that we are "made in the image of God" — so we have, of course, forgotten who the other is as well.

Sabbath says that we are accountable for the way we live our lives, the way we do or do not develop our humanity, the way we allow the abuse of others in our name.

Sabbath says that we are made for reflection and that unless we do it, unless we begin to reflect on what we are doing as humans to other humans, to the earth, to the cosmos, we become nothing but cogs in an enslaving system.

Sabbath says that time is the only resource we really have and that we must teach ourselves to use it well.

Jesus, scripture is clear, kept the Jewish Sabbath. But Christians, as time went by, found themselves further and further from the synagogue. At first pious Jews in a Jewish culture, they gradually came to see themselves as a very separate Jewish sect. At the same time, as Jews began to suspect their messianism, Christians, especially the Christians outside of Jerusalem, became more and more Christ-centered, more and more committed to Jesus as the messiah.

For Christians, then, for clearly theological reasons, "Sabbath" became "Sunday" by the second, third, and fourth centuries. The life of Jesus was its centerpiece. Resurrection trumped death and life was eternal. But the concept remained the same: life was not to be taken lightly, not to be taken for granted. Regular reflection on its meaning, its purpose gave it unending energy, renewed direction. Sunday Sabbath for the Christian meant celebration, yes, but it also meant "remembrance."

It is the remembrance of who we are, what we are about, why we were made that we all need again in a world that at times seems to be plummeting toward its own devastation, both internal and external. Sabbath is the centerpiece of life, the keystone of its development, the key to its meaning, the path to its future.

Loss of Sabbath time in the modern world may be an ominous signal. The twenty-four-hour day, seven-day week makes it possible for people who work during the traditional business hours of past eras to do their shopping, get to the dentist, get technical support in off-hours. But as good, as necessary, as that may be, what provides now for the building up of the Sabbath-heart? And it is the Sabbath-heart that is really needed if, as a culture, we are going to make good decisions about the rest of life, the important things of life.

It is the promptings of the Sabbath-heart that remind us to do justice to the rest of world.

Sabbath says everything all the grandmothers of an earlier age were trying to teach us: be still, be thoughtful, be contented, be gentle with the world and you will become everything you were ever meant to be.

And then . . .

When I was growing up, I got the distinct idea that to "keep holy the Sabbath" meant to go to church. Now I have come to realize that it means a great deal more than that.

I remember the situation very clearly. I was in Jerusalem for the first time. The occasion was an international meeting of professional women, but, as far as I was concerned, the more important thing was that it gave me a chance to see the Holy Land. Anything else was pure bonus.

Because it was Friday, the beginning of the Jewish Sabbath, the first order of the day for our Jewish hostesses was the Shabbat meal, and we were all invited. I would learn as much that way about Jewish culture and society, I figured, as I possibly could at the lectures.

What I did not realize was that the Shabbat meal was a great deal more than the meal. It was really a Shabbat event. In the first place, we could not drive a car to the synagogue; we would have to walk. Orthodox Jews do not use equipment on Shabbat. In the second place, the regular elevator in the hotel would not run after sundown. We would have to walk up the stairs or cross the hotel lobby to use "the Shabbat elevator" that was reserved for guests. Finally, the only hot food that would be served for breakfast until Shabbat ended on Saturday evening would be hot coffee and tea that would be made in cauldrons on electric timers. Clearly, everything — everything — stopped on the Sabbath in Jerusalem.

It was all a little stringent, I thought. Maybe even exaggerated. After all, the commandment says "keep holy the Sabbath," not "stop everything on the Sabbath." Given the current Christian notion that keeping the Sabbath means attending church services, the whole notion of simply halting life as we know it made no sense. To what use? After all, Sabbath and life are two different things, aren't they?

But then the rabbi got up to explain Shabbat to the guests. "The Talmud," he said, "gives us three reasons for keeping the Sabbath:

"The first reason for Sabbath," he went on, "is that given the fact that no one is permitted to do anything on Shabbat, no orders could be given, no work done. Therefore, the slaves and the rich would be equal for at least one day a week.

"The second reason is that we have time to reflect on the meaning of our lives.

"The third reason for Sabbath is that we can reflect on the goodness of our work as God did on creation on the seventh day."

Nice, I thought. But does it really translate to our world here and now? Is it practical? Does it even make sense?

Then, just before he sat down, he did something that took Shabbat out of the Talmud and put it right in the middle of life. "See this pen," he said twirling a fountain pen between his fingers. "I am a writer. This is my work." He took his pen and put it in his briefcase. "On Shabbat," he finished, "I never use a pen. Today is for God and me. Not for me." That one I understood.

A week later, I returned to the States. On Sunday morning, after Mass, the streets were teeming with cars, all the stores were open, lawn mowers roared on every street while people did what they hadn't had time to do during the week, office lights blinked on, the city was alive with business. I sat in the midst of it all thinking of the years in my grandmother's house when no work was allowed on Sunday. "Quaint," I thought — and sadly, sadly missing.

Surely the real sin to which the third commandment points is not the sin of not going to church on Sunday. It is the sin of not seriously seeking God.

And for you...

The world has lost a Sabbath mentality. Now Sunday is not about "keeping holy the Lord's day"; it's about catching up on what we didn't get finished on the weekdays before it.

Sabbath rituals are those sacred forms of life that enable us to transcend time for the sake of a glimpse of eternity. Then daily life ceases to be humdrum and the fear, the desperation, of death washes away.

"Ritual is the way we carry the presence of the sacred," Christina Baldwin says. "Ritual is the spark that must not go out." When we forego the rituals that link us to the divine, we reduce all of life to the mundane. We not only lose our way home; we run the risk of forgetting that there is a home beyond this one.

"Sunday," Yoshiko Uchida writes, "is sort of like a piece of bright gold brocade lying in a pile of white muslin weekdays." Sabbath is the light that keeps us moving through darkness to the great sunrise we do not know but cannot even imagine doubting.

We have made the Sabbath one more thing on the schedule rather than a celebration of those moments in life that transcend the schedule and free us from the slavery of schedule.

Time study research tells us that Americans work 350 more hours or nine work weeks more than the average European per year. The same studies tell us that Americans suffer more from stress, cardiac arrest, hardening of the arteries, and cancer than Europeans do. Maybe in a capitalist world, Sabbath is an idea whose time has come.

Sabbath is not about church: it is about contemplation of the important things in life, the things of the soul. "People whose religion begins and ends with worship and ritual practices," Mordecai Kaplan wrote, "are like soldiers forever maneuvering, but never getting into action." Sabbath never ends in church. It only begins there.

A Sabbath heart is what happens in us when we make room for God in life. Then the quiet and space that come from putting down today in order to live in the realm of the eternal enables us to move into a sense of the presence of God that is not strained, or forced, or affected. Sabbath is what brings us to a consciousness of the divine in the human enterprise.

Sabbath is the healer of relationships. Just as the rich had to recognize the humanity of the slave on the Sabbath, so does Sabbath give us the opportunity to look at the quality of our own bonds, both inside and outside of the family, to make them real and equal and just.

By ignoring the Sabbath, we turn every day of life into an average day, a routine day, a working day. We lose a sense of celebration. We forget to stop and enjoy the world as God enjoyed creation. Scripture is clear: "And God looked and saw that it was good."

Shabbat reminds us that we are part of the human community, which is why we gather with the community of faith. We gather to revive those connections and to remember those responsibilities and to be supported in those efforts.

Ritual oils the soul with the familiar invitation to step into the arms of God and out of the tentacles of anything lesser.

Fourth

THE LAW OF CARING

Honor your father and your mother.
— Exodus 20:12

In the beginning...

"When a sage dies, the whole world mourns," the Talmud teaches. The lesson, embedded in the Ten Commandments, begs for rediscovery in a culture in which ageism threatens to rob us of wisdom, and families are scattered from one end of the world to the other.

The fourth commandment asks us to look again at the way we care for those who, having gone before us, show us the way. It reminds us, at the same time, of our own debt to generations to come.

The funeral rituals of Judaism — some of them as old as Judaism itself, all of them still part of today's Jewish burial services — do as much to underscore the profound meaning of the fourth commandment as any lecture on creation ever could. Three of them, in particular, shed new light on the relationships between one generation and another.

First, in the Jewish tradition, a dead body is considered equivalent to a damaged Torah scroll. It is no longer able to fulfill the purpose for which it was created, but it is to be reverenced for the holy purpose it once served. In recognition of the contribution the deceased made to life, the body is never left unattended from the moment of death to the burial service. It is what we learn from those before us that enables us to go forward fearlessly ourselves.

Second, kaddish, the Jewish prayer that affirms life and reiterates a person's faith and acceptance of God's will, is said daily for eleven months — minus one day for parents to signify that the very act of parenthood is itself a holy and meritorious act that renders the fullness of the normal penitential period following death unnecessary. Parenting, we learn, transcends the value to the children alone. It is a holy gift for the sake of the whole human community.

Third, the celebration of Avelut — the twelve-month mourning period prescribed for parents in many Jewish communities — exceeds the mourning period defined for any other relationship, including one's spouse. Those who bring us into the world, who participate in the co-creation of the universe, we come to understand, deserve our special care, our special reverence, our special acknowledgment.

In Judaism, as in Christianity, death is a celebration of life, but the lives of those who bore and raised us have a claim on society itself that is immense in its implications.

Yahwism is not an ethereal religion. It does not live in the realm of the airy-fairy. Human beings are made of "dust," Genesis teaches. They belong to the earth (Gen. 2:7). There is no escaping it in drugs or trances, fantasy or illusion. Yahwism faces life straight on and head up. The here-and-now is its only raw material. Yahwists have no other realm in which to function. Unlike the followers of other religions of the Middle East, they do not posit a world beyond this one. All they know for sure is here. It is here that meaning takes place, that God acts, that humans become fully human.

The Israelite, then, values life with peculiar intensity. The Israelite wishes to die "old and full of days." Premature and sudden death is considered a divine punishment, in fact (Ps. 102). This God is "the God of the living," not of the dead. Beyond this life might be existence, yes, but an existence more marked by darkness and oblivion than by energy and joy (Ps. 88).

No wonder then that the commandments single out for special consideration those parents and elderly, the sages of our lives, who have cared for us and now need our care in return.

And yet, here in our own land, where people have waged legal battles in the Supreme Court about the place of images and artifacts of the Ten Commandments on public buildings and in government facilities, the government claiming to be organized under those same commandments and the Judeo-Christian tradition is forever fashioning plans to circumscribe, to scuttle, to trim, to limit the kind of care we give to those who have worked all their lives and then cannot care for themselves.

As families get smaller and offspring take up residence half a world away, the whole notion of what happens to an older generation left alone, left penniless, becomes a larger question than ever before in recorded history. It has serious implications for the fourth commandment.

Workers, some financial planners tell us, should develop their own retirement monies rather than depend on government programs as they get older.

Interestingly enough, surveys have shown that more younger workers than older people approve of the plan. Young and ambitious, weaned on the promise of eternal progress and sure of their own health and financial prowess, they are sure they can do better handling their own money, make themselves a larger retirement pension, than any government system based on income levels will do for them.

Older people, on the other hand, know that private investment, even if they have anything to invest, is at best a flimsy plan. They have seen, over the years, that stock values come and go, mutual funds fail, companies rise and fall in their profit margins. They know they will be affected by all those things when they are too old to do anything about them. Worse than that, they fear that no one else will be around who will do anything to help them either.

Those who work at low-income jobs all their lives know that they will have little or no money to invest to begin with. Their old age is doomed to long working years, no retirement time, or desperate poverty.

Is this kind of care for an elderly generation in the spirit of a commandment that calls a people to "honor their parents"?

In early Israel, tribes were divided into clans and clans into families and the family was the mainstay of the society. Tradition, ancestors, lineage gave a person a strong sense of identity. It also provided the kind of support system that our own world of small, far-flung nuclear families cannot provide in the average family. Our answer to the fragmentation of the modern family has been public institutions, some of them subsidized, most of them not.

It is a far cry from the social system implied in the fourth commandment. It is even further afield of Judaism's reverence for its sages.

Underneath the Israelite view of life runs one unyielding theme: human beings — both women and men — are only "slightly lower than the angels." Both women and men are "made in the image of God."

Both women and men, then, have dignity, have rights, have value.

No one can simply be thrown away as useless, a common practice in some ancient societies when food became scarce or the elderly became a physical burden. To be family, after all, is to be in relationships that are continuous and permanent, not discrete and temporary.

It is a crucial social issue, this implication of what it means to be family — to be concerned for the place of acumen and wisdom in a culture. It is an insight too often disregarded in a society so highly technical that yesterday's knowledge is considered obsolete and a lifetime of discernment is often considered useless.

More than ignore the wisdom generations before us have to bring to the questions of the time as they get older, though, this society tends to emphasize the role of family background in every person's life in ways that lead to either self-denigration or self-glorification. Either we learn to deny who we are and where we came from and what all that means to the development of both strengths and weaknesses in us, or we will learn to exaggerate the effects of our parentage and family relationships to the point that we take as our own identity the honor earned for us by our ancestors. We begin to be who we came from and refuse to take responsibility to become who we see in them we must be.

But, the fourth commandment reminds us, we are not worlds unto ourselves. We all came from somebody somewhere and we owe them the gratitude that comes with those gifts, however limited they may at first sight seem to be.

It is the requirement of this commandment that saves us from the terminal disease of immediacy. This commandment demands that we respect the past. It keeps us in touch with our roots. It forces us to remember what we are most likely — even most eager — to forget. It refuses to allow us to discard yesterday in favor of a present dedicated to the glorification of the self.

In Israel, the debt to the past was paid through reverence for the debt we owe our parents — and, in fact, the accumulated wisdom of all the generations before us.

The fourth commandment builds perspective into the human race. It is not simply a mandate to remember the past but to be aware through it of our own responsibility to the future. We are the sages of tomorrow, we come to realize. What we leave future generations can only be what we have made of ourselves and passed on to them. What we leave them will mark their own lives: enormous debt, nuclear bombs, racial violence, religious intolerance. Whatever we leave undone, they will bear.

We learn by being confronted every day with the heritage we bear from ages before us. As the Native Americans say: no decision should be made without considering its effect up to the seventh generation.

We learn to consider the past seriously and the future thoughtfully. We learn to understand that what we do now will also impact the future, just as the lives and decisions of our own ancestors affected us. We rediscover the world's need for sages.

This commandment is the call to bring new respect to the intergenerational connections this society stands so near to the brink of losing. As the Jewish proverb says: "The only truly dead are those who have been forgotten."

And then...

In Oslo I walked through one of the most impacting statuary gardens in the world. Sculpted by Norway's premier sculptor, Gustav Vigeland, the 121 larger-than-life pieces depict the full range of human life and family, from infancy to old age. They stretch across the river bridge from one side to the other on both sides of a four-lane highway that connects one part of the park to the other.

Called *The Cycle of Life,* the work traces the coming together of a young couple, the coming of their children, then the changing relationship of parent and child. Finally, the artist shows us the connection between the generations: a grandfather and a grandson, a grandmother and a little girl. You can't help stare in awe at some of the huge pieces, find tears in your eyes at the sight of others. A walk across the bridge is a walk through your own life. If you watch the people watching the statues, as well as the statues themselves, you get glimpses of the pain and the beauty that underlie each of their separate lives at separate stages.

But one of the statues on the garden bridge stops every sightseer in their tracks. To this one, the response is almost always universal delight. This one is the Sinnetagen, the figure of a foot-stomping, raging two-year-old who is claiming his right to be human, to be listened to, to be respected for who he is and what he wants.

This particular statue, I think, tells the whole story of the fourth commandment. The fourth commandment is not about acquiescence of powerless children to the will of authoritarian parents. It is about being allowed to test ourselves against the world under the eye and with the wisdom of those who, loving us, have gone the way before.

At this point in my own life, two things strike me about this commandment. First, it seems to be totally out of place in the list. Second, it leaves out the other half of the equation: Why doesn't it say anything about what parents should do?

I think the answers lie in the fact that this commandment is really much broader than it seems at first sight. It talks about much more than what we hear at a first reading of it. The fourth commandment is not simply about children. Nor is it only about "parents," in the strict biological sense of the word. This commandment is about cherishing the gift of human relationships.

The first three commandments deal with reverence for God. The last six deal with justice among people. Only the fourth deals with relationships of love, the commandment to care. This one we all thought we understood. I wonder.

The fourth commandment tells us to honor whatever it is, whoever it is whose place in our life has been a place of honor, the ones who brought us to growth, to wholeness of life, the ones whose ways have given direction to our own. And they have done it, the Sinnetagen reminds us, not by trying to own us or control us or frighten us with their "authority" but by giving us the space, the patience and the love that enables us to come to grips with our raging, petulant, narcissistic self.

Honor your father and your mother. Honor those who are parenting your soul to wholeness.

Honor all of those parental figures who brought you beyond self-centeredness to the decent human self you are today.

And for you . . .

To force my will on others is not to form them; it is simply to control them. That is not parenting. That is egotism. Anne Bradstreet wrote years ago: "Authority without wisdom is like a heavy axe without an edge; fitter to bruise than polish."

People learn by being allowed to make mistakes. Pity the child of perfect parents. Pity the parents who think that perfection is either attainable or desirable.

Each of us, whether we have children or not, gives birth to the next generation. We do it by being either wise or foolish, loving or hostile, arrogant or humble in their presence.

No parents are typical. No parents are perfect. We do not honor them for that. We honor them because they did what they could in making us what we are. The rest we were meant to do for ourselves.

Those who have parented us in life are those we carry inside ourselves forever. They deserve to be brought out into the light so that others, too, can bask in their ongoing glory — this time in us.

No wonder "honor" is a commandment. Not to honor those who have carried us through any part of life is a sin against the Creator who goes on creating us through the work of others. "Without feelings of respect," Confucius said, "what is there to distinguish men and women from beasts?"

The fourth commandment teaches us not to take love for granted ourselves. We know we've grown up when we begin to say thank you to those who stood by while we got there. To leave those thank-yous unsaid is to be unnecessarily hurtful. "How sharper than a serpent's tooth it is," Shakespeare reminds us, "to have a thankless child."

If we never defied the people who parented us, either we never really grew up or they never really allowed it. "Parents," Peter Ustinov wrote, "are the bones on which children sharpen their teeth."

To have authority over others does not mean to have control of them. It means simply that we must have love for them. Or as Garrison Keillor says it: "Parents should sit tall in the saddle and look upon their troops with a noble and benevolent and extremely nearsighted gaze." Don't see too much or you will spoil their opportunity to see it themselves.

Being older than someone else or in a higher position than someone else does not endow us with eternal truth. It simply means that we must learn to listen with a wiser ear. The Jewish proverb reads: "The ancient authorities are entitled to a vote, but not to a veto."

The purpose of "parenting," of companioning the young, the novice, the stranger through the traces of life

is not to make them dependent. It is to make them inde-
pendent. The purpose of parenting is to make ourselves
unnecessary. "I am not you anymore." Saundra Sharp
wrote, "I am my own collection of gifts and errors."

We can never give too much honor to those who
have saved us from ourselves. "My mother," Sharon
Doubtiago wrote, "is a poem I'll never be able to write /
though everything I write is a poem to my mother."

Fifth

THE LAW OF LIFE

You shall not kill.
— Exodus 20:13

In the beginning…

While we sit and watch the news at night, the world around us — unarmed and undefended — is being pummeled to the point of extinction. What is the moral answer to such a situation at a time when raw power rampages across the globe undeterred? Sixty percent of all the war deaths of all time, in fact, did not happen in ancient civilizations at the hands of uncivilized people. They happened in the twentieth century.

What does the tradition say about those things? How, if at all, are the Ten Commandments a guide through an era such as this?

"To save one life," the Talmud teaches, "is to save the world." Those who value life in small ways, the teaching implies, create a culture of life around them that calls the rest of us to examine our own attitudes about life. They save the world from unconsciously accepting the kind of violence that, in the long run, would only destroy it in some kind of distorted quest for good. By using violence to stop violence, only new violence can possibly be created. And so we become bloodthirsty in the name of goodness and God.

The fifth commandment, the word of life, calls us to remember how thin a line we tread between potency and power, between power and force.

It calls us to choose carefully the kinds of power we opt to exercise.

"Power," the Talmud teaches, "buries those who wield it." Such a warning for peoples, countries, cultures up to their neck in power has no small meaning in the modern world. Power, once personal, has become global. Once a matter of charism or physical strength, personal charm or public position, in our time power has become the capacity to move systems: political and military, economic or social. It is the power to wield power without compunction, without control.

In its midst, the fifth commandment stands in mute condemnation of those for whom life is cheap and death is called life-giving.

The problem is that power, ruthlessly employed, carelessly administered, often masks as virtue, often wantonly destroys in its determination to do good. The United States, for instance, one of only fourteen countries in the world that has reinstated capital punishment, is so sure of its criminal justice system that it cavalierly dismisses its "mistakes" as the price to be paid for "deterrence."

The fifth commandment warns us against our willingness, our ability, to bring things down on the heads of others in the name of righteousness. In the end, our anger, our force, our murderous impulses make things happen that do more harm than good.

The Hebrew scriptures, on which the Judeo-Christian tradition rests yet today, took over a thousand years to develop. That entire period, as well as the time from then to now, has been spent in interpretation, commentary, and exegesis. Ideas taken for granted in one segment of the Bible — the way the community was to deal with slaves, for instance — becomes suspect in another.

The fifth commandment, astonishing for its simplicity in some ways, maddening for its confusion in others, has been at least as complex in its implications as any of the others. Maybe even more so.

Grounded in the basic Hebraic principle of the dignity of life, the glory of having been created "in God's image," the fifth commandment would seem to be a straightforward affirmation of the sanctity of human life. But the Bible itself is full of killing and the list of crimes for which the scriptures imposed the death penalty — violation of the Sabbath, adultery, bestiality, homosexuality, and sacrifice to other gods, as well as murder — is troublesome.

Issues common to our own time make us revisit all the old questions — and add a few more of our own.

Every age before us has wrestled with the problem. The Marquis de Sade, in the eighteenth century, challenges the very notion of state killing or capital punishment, for instance. He says, "Murder is a horror, but an often necessary horror, never criminal, which it is essential to tolerate. . . . Is it or is it not a crime? If it is not, why make laws for its punishment? And if it is, by what barbarous logic do you, to punish it, duplicate it by another crime?"

In our own century, the questions are even more pointed, more divisive. Some Christian groups call abortion "murder," but Jewish groups do not. Some people call war "justified," but some Christian groups do not. Some people call capital punishment a "deterrent," but others call it barbarous.

The question is why? Why this much confusion over something that seems so "normal," so common? We find ourselves at war regularly. We identify "capital crimes" for the sake of social order regularly. We believe in "self-defense." What can possibly be the problem here?

The issue is a crucial one. It depends on what we really mean by the fifth commandment and it depends on what we really think, as Christians, that Jesus was really all about.

The problem introduced by the fifth commandment rests on the continually developing Jewish interpretation of it. The issue has always revolved around a matter of translation. The question is whether or not the fifth commandment is "You shall not kill" or "You shall not murder." The distinction is determinative.

"Kill" — from *harag* in Hebrew — is a comprehensive term that includes the taking of life for all reasons and in all forms. "Murder" — from *ratsah* in Hebrew — refers only to criminal acts of killing. Early translations of the scriptures used the word "kill," but, as time went by, these translations were contested. Respected Jewish scholars argued that the words used in the original rendering of the commandment meant to reflect a concept that was much narrower than that. A great deal of killing is necessary, they insisted, and not criminal at all.

On the other hand, Rabbi Maimonides, the Thomas Aquinas of twelfth-century Judaism, wrote that all cases of killing human beings involve violations of the command, even if the violation happens to be overridden by other mitigating factors, such as unprovoked attack, for instance. Maimonides brooked no arguments about "mitigating" factors in interpreting God's will for the world. Every instance of killing violated the Jewish commitment to life.

The argument has raged for years and rages on in contemporary society still. Jewish scholars themselves continue to debate the topic.

But even for those who accept the notion that the commandment forbids only criminal killing, the list of offenses that purported to justify capital punishment in Judaism has changed considerably through the ages. Sorcerers, blasphemers, those who curse their parents, rebellious elders, and those who break the laws governing the Sabbath have come off the list.

As the consciousness of the Hebrew community grew spiritually, psychologically, socially, and scientifically about the entire dynamic of human motives and human harm, so did the consciousness of the community about its own moral responsibility to life and nonviolent forms of punishment.

For Christians, the struggle became even more troubling. Jesus, the revolutionary, revolted against an entire worldview peacefully, lovingly, and nonviolently. "Peter, put away your sword," he said to those who would have defended him against arrest, imprisonment, and eventual crucifixion by a Roman legion in Jewish Palestine.

Early Christian history up to the time of Constantine, too, stands as a stark reminder of the more pacifist position of the early church when Christians did not join the army and would not take up arms to defend the Roman Empire or sacrifice to Roman gods.

In our own time, the question has emerged even more fiercely. Can a war ever be "just" in a nuclear age when there is no distinction between combatants and noncombatants and the very thought of nuclear weaponry destroys any notion of either proportionality or "winning." Is abortion "murder" if we have no scientific consensus on the meaning of life? Is stem-cell research the destruction of life? Is the elimination of the feeding tubes of terminally ill patients really "euthanasia"? And who decides — and how?

So what is the fifth commandment saying to us at this point in history while our own definitions of life and capital offenses are shifting, just as they did over time for the Jewish community itself?

Maybe it says the simplest and most profound thing of all. Maybe it simply says that life is worth struggling for, worth struggling over, worth struggling to define. Maybe it is telling us that peace is our only real defense now. Maybe it is telling us that failing to support the families and children of our society with health care, housing, food, education, day care, and just wages — the things that constitute the essentials of the dignified human life — is at least as much a sin against life as war, abortion, euthanasia, and stem-cell therapy will ever be.

"If murder is forgiven, heaven will find it hard to bear," the Chinese proverb teaches. The fifth commandment requires us to determine when, if ever, heaven will not weep over our own disregard of life.

And then...

The third Parliament of the World's Religions, which was held in Cape Town, South Africa, in 1999, brought over four hundred religious leaders from every religious denomination on earth together. The first parliament, convened in Chicago in 1893, despite its clear success, never met again for a hundred years, thanks to a century of bloody wars and political fault lines.

When, finally, another generation of religious leaders, still living in the memory of that first historic convention, decided to hold a second global assembly in 1993, one of the major decisions of the group was that they would meet every few years thereafter.

Clearly, the intent of the members of the Parliament of the World's Religions was not to be a religious bazaar of exotic rituals and robes where the people of the world could come and take samplings of belief systems and then, like buyers at a food fair, decide which suited best their varied tastes. These spiritual leaders were about far greater things than that. They were serious about the role of religion in human affairs, about the creation of a common spiritual climate, about being part of the resolution of world conflict rather than a seedbed for it as has been the case for so many generations now.

One of the major acts of the third assembly, therefore, was to stress the common ground among the world's religions rather than their innate tensions and differences.

But I had grown up in a "mixed marriage." The very concept of common ground and single vision among the religions of the world was light years away from even the very simple Catholic/Protestant divide in which I myself had been raised. I couldn't help but wonder what would really happen when someone tried such a thing.

There aren't many times in life when a person can see one world ending and another about to begin, but I knew in that assembly that day that it had happened to me.

I was there when they read and accepted "The Global Ethic," which affirmed the unity of world religions around four central ethical principles. I could almost feel the breath of the Holy Spirit vibrating in the assembly.

One thing they were sure of was that "you shall not kill."

Life, every religion in the world said, was to be affirmed, protected, honored, and sustained.

The commitment was to far more than simply "not killing." The commitment was to enabling.

I couldn't help but wonder whether we hadn't been misrepresenting and manipulating the fifth commandment for a long, long time. After all, of all the commandments, it's the one we keep least carefully, most cavalierly. We make up reasons all the time to kill: we kill to preserve the state; we kill to protect the self; we kill to punish wrongdoers — a silly concept if ever there was one. After all, who gets "punished," let alone rehabilitated, once we kill a wrongdoer? We kill to enforce authority. We kill for political reasons. And, finally, we kill whole segments of society — strip their lands, rape their forests, soil their air — to satisfy whole other segments of society. "You shall not kill"? Hardly.

Maybe it's time to look at the fifth commandment from the other side of it.

Maybe it's time to realize that when we are not actively working to sustain life, all life anywhere, we are actually undermining life everywhere.

"You shall not kill" must become "You shall enable life" before it's too late for the entire globe. Life is the only thing of value we really have. And we kill it in so many ways for so many bad reasons.

And for you...

When one part of life dies in us, or is taken from us, it is resurrection time. "Life is a series of little deaths," Charles Feidelson Jr. wrote, "out of which life always returns." It's about allowing life to return in us after loss and disappointment or natural endings and social failures that the fifth commandment is also about.

When we spend life on something that will outlast it — the family, life issues themselves, lost values — death, even when it comes, is never final.

When we eat and smoke and drink to excess, exactly those things that are slowly killing us, we are ignoring the full moral message of what it means to be told "you shall not kill."

Medicare and Social Security and food stamps and unemployment compensation are not simply "social programs." They are the very essence of what it means to sustain life for others, to refuse to kill, to make life livable for everyone. "Woe to the hand," Shakespeare wrote, "that shed this costly blood." Maybe we should think of that when we're making decisions about social policies.

We kill what we do not allow to develop. "You cannot shake hands," Indira Gandhi said, "with a clenched fist." To attack someone is to destroy whatever the future might have held for us if we had chosen to nourish life instead of destroy it.

Physical death is far more kind than the smothering of the spirit that comes with rejection, distance, disinterest. Physical death only ends physical life. Spiritual wounding takes away the joy that life should bring.

The greatest sin against the fifth commandment, "You shall not kill," may be indifference to what is going on that is sapping life out of the world around us.

When I care enough about something to want to save it rather than to end it, I have come to the real meaning of creation. "The salvation of humankind," Solzhenitsyn wrote, "lies only in making everything the concern of all."

Of course "You shall not kill" is a daily problem. "All of us are responsible for one another," the Talmud teaches. And people are dying before their time everywhere in the world. I must do something about that—even if it is only to say it.

The life that we fail to enable and sustain we condemn to death. And all the time we think that this is a commandment that has nothing to do with us.

Sometimes we kill the future before it comes. We decide that at a certain age, a given stage in life, living will be over. That's euthanasia of the soul. Every period of life has something new to offer. Don't kill it off before it even gets here.

We can't always make sense out of our life. We can even wish it over sometimes. But when we do that it is only a sign that we have yet to learn to see life as a whole. "Life is an unanswered question," Tennessee Williams wrote, "but let's still believe in the dignity and importance of the question."

Sixth

THE LAW OF COMMITMENT

You shall not commit adultery.

—Exodus 20:14

In the beginning...

The problem with the sixth commandment — "You shall not commit adultery" — is that no one in the Hebrew scriptures seems to keep it. Solomon, Israel's first and most revered king, a model of wisdom, the exemplar of justice, had seven hundred wives. What's more, the scripture is clear, he was not punished because he had more than one wife; he was punished because many of his wives were foreigners and had brought their idols with them to his palace.

In fact, the Hebrew scriptures are full of adulterous relationships, it seems — even by the most exalted of biblical figures. Jacob married both Leah and Rachel. David took Bathsheba from Uriah, the commander of his own army. Elkinah loved one of his wives —

Hannah — more than he loved the other, Penninah. Abraham took Hagar as concubine. And because Onan refused to sleep with his dead brother's wife so that she could have children in her husband's name — what Israel called a "levirate marriage" — Yahweh killed him. Clearly, polygyny, concubinage, and levirate assignations were not only common; they were legal.

So is this the commandment no one paid any attention to or is this the commandment that had no value?

What are we to think about a commandment that not only was not kept but whose aberrations were institutionalized? What "word" can it possibly be for us if it had no meaning even to Israel itself? How can it possibly say anything to us about the good life, about morality, about goodness?

Two places that appear to offer little understanding of the sixth commandment in the context of contemporary culture are the Bible and the Talmud, though each of them states the principle clearly and without mitigation.

In the Bible, adultery does not have to do with the violation of intimacy or trust or relationship or love. It has to do with property law and inheritance. In the Talmud it has to do with family order and harmony.

And yet, underneath these very diverse — and, in some ways, even shocking — renderings of what we think adultery is all about, lie some very important principles, some very humanizing insights, some very spiritual dimensions of life. Despite all the different ways in which marriage was practiced and defined in the

Hebrew scriptures — all of them different from ours, all of them considered immoral by us, in fact — some very clear constants exist. Marriage, as Israel knew it, may not have been based on "love" as we define it, but it was based on clearly outlined conditions. Man and wife had responsibilities for one another and they were expected to keep them. "Love," by and large, was not the definition of Hebrew marriage. It was duty, obligation, and responsibility that measured its morality, its depth, its value, its worth.

In biblical law, the idea of adultery is very different for men than for women. In the first place, where men were concerned, adultery had nothing whatsoever to do with monogamy. On the contrary, according to biblical law, polygyny, the right for a man to have more than one wife, was taken for granted. Wives and children were a measure of his wealth, a promise of his future security.

Adultery, then, had nothing to do with a man's having sexual relations with multiple wives or unmarried women. It had something do with having sexual relations with another man's wife. Another man's property.

Wives were owned, not simply "married." They were for assuring the lines of inheritance and the lineage of the clan. They were for keeping the bloodlines pure and the property of the clan intact. For one man to threaten the purity of another man's lineage undermined the integrity, even the wealth, of the family line.

An adulterous woman, on the other hand, was a married woman who had sexual relations with any man, married or single, not her husband. She would be punished, divorced, or even stoned to death. Polyandry — the taking of more than one husband — was absolutely forbidden. Sex, it seems, was, by and large, a woman's sin.

In fact, Rabbinic law decreed that four wives ought to be the maximum for any man. More than that, the rabbis declared, would be difficult to sustain since some of them would be given less attention than others. Consciousness of the negative effect on women themselves as persons emerged only gradually.

Eventually, of course, here as in all other institutions, the interpretations of the rabbis modified the more ancient marriage practices and their effects on women, but, through it all, marriage remained a basically male institution throughout the ages.

So what is to be gained here that can possibly give new spirit to our own age in a culture where almost one out of every two marriages now ends in divorce? What does the sixth commandment have to say to us about the fabric of our own society when we do not marry for the sake of inheritance or family perpetuity? What "word" can we hear to find meaning for our own time under such a stark command: You shall not commit adultery.

The word implied by the sixth commandment in this age, it seems, is commitment. In an age that is less and less stable about anything, feels less and less responsible for anything beyond the present, marriage is one of the few institutions based on perpetuity. On singleness of heart. On mutual trust.

Everything else in modern life is a movable feast. Today people are born in one state, raised in a second, go to school in a third, marry and raise their own families in a fourth, retire in a fifth, and are buried in a sixth. Families are dispersed across the country, around the world. Family ties are stretched to the limit, blended, ended, and, unless we work at our relationships very hard, reduced to names on a Christmas card list or lost entirely. Then if the commandments mean anything to us at all, "You shall not commit adultery" brings us back to the notion of permanence, of what it means to be family, of the spiritual meaning of the constancy of relationships.

In this day and age, we do not marry for the sake of property and clans, perhaps, but we are keenly aware of the need for human intimacy in this time of empty crowds. Everywhere we go we are surrounded by thousands of strangers at one time, none of whom, we know down deep, really care if we are there or not. The world is a great, gaping, vacuous place where we are doomed to insignificance until we are significant to someone else.

Marriage is about eternal human significance. It is not about sex, not about sexism, not about ownership, not about security. It is about finding what is missing in ourselves and providing what is missing in another until, because of that, both of us can become who we are really meant to be. Adultery is seldom what really destroys a relationship. Adultery is often what signals that the relationship has already deteriorated. Then we realize that the relationship, the love, must go beyond sex to intimacy.

That takes time. That takes patience. That takes trust. That takes honesty. That takes forgiveness. That takes emotional stability. That takes surrender to the process of growth.

To violate that process affects not only the couple themselves but the entire community of which they are a part. It interrupts the process of growth. It disturbs relationships everywhere. It barters the security and identity of the children. It makes any relationship in the future a risk.

The fact is that we all seek relationships because none of us is self-sufficient. Each of us dies the death of the soul alone. Only by giving ourselves into the care of another for the sake of the other can we ever become fully known, fully challenged, fully human.

Disregard for the relationship, exploitation of the partnership, narcissistic victimization of another — sexually, emotionally, psychologically — for the sake of the self is a violation of the sixth commandment. It is sexual abuse of the worst kind.

The capacity to form and maintain relationships is one of the signs of mental health, of psychological maturity, of the ability to respond empathically.

Unless we are able to feel the feelings of another, we are doomed to go through life concentrating solely on the self. Our world narrows simply to the breadth of our own concerns. Our perspective shrinks to the level of the narcissistic. We lose a vision of the wider world. We define the rest of the world according to our own interests alone. And those we pursue with little or no concern for the concerns or feelings of others. We become a world unto ourselves.

It is the narcissistic personality that is capable of the most heinous of behaviors, the most pathological of social actions. It is not that the great social deviants of the world — Hitler, Goering, Goebbels, Stalin, Nero, Claudius — were insane. The problem is that they were narcissists. They loved no one but themselves.

Love that lasts, that invests itself in the welfare of another, is the only human proof we have of the nature of the God who is "with us all days," who is constant and worthy of love, who wants our "weal and not our woe," whose constancy we can count on.

"You shall not commit adultery" is the word that calls us to truly care about the people we say we love. Not to use them. Not to exploit them. Not to ignore them. Not to patronize them. Not to manipulate them for the sake of our own satisfaction. People are not toys or trophies to be collected and abandoned. The people we love are those to whom we commit our lives, entrust our futures, and share our selves so that both we and they — they and we — can grow into fully loving people. In this relationship, two equals are meant to become more together than they ever could be alone. That is the intimacy that cannot be compromised — that cannot be abused — if we ourselves are, as the Hebrews knew in their eternal contract with one another, ever really to become whole.

And then...

The Hindus tell a story that may say more about the real meaning of the sixth commandment than we might at first glance imagine.

Once upon a time, the story goes, a disciple wanted very much to give up his life in the world and become a renunciate, a not unusual religious discipline in that culture. The problem, he explained, was that his wife and family loved him too much to let him go.

"Love?" his guru said. "That isn't love at all. Love frees. Listen. . . . " And he gave the disciple a yogic secret that would enable him to simulate the state of death.

The next day the man was dead to all outward appearances and the house trembled with the cries and wailing of the family.

Then the guru showed up and told the weeping family that he had the power to bring the man back to life if only someone could be found to die in the disciple's place. Any volunteers?

To the "corpse's" astonishment, every member of the family began to explain why it was necessary to keep their own lives. Finally, the corpse's wife said, "There's really no need for anyone to take his place. We'll manage without him."

Adultery is when we take someone else's life and love, use them up, and then go on our own way "managing without them." It's not love at all: it's exploitation. It's release without relationship.

We treat the sixth commandment as if it were about physical misbehavior. But that may be the least of the problem. The sixth commandment is about integrity of heart, about loving people more spiritually than we insist on loving them physically. Adultery is the state of using people for personal physical satisfaction, without intention of commitment, without being willing to die in their place. "No strings attached," we call it, meaning no promises made, no obligations assumed, no complementarity. No real bonding, just reflex action that is as much outside of us as inside of us.

The sixth commandment is not about not loving. It is about loving rightly, meaning loving with the soul as well as with the body. It is about saving us from the pitfalls of passion without the presence of the fullness of the self.

We have a lot of body love going on in the United States today. It's not clear, however, how much of that love started in the heart, rests in the soul, and is simply expressed by the body.

This is the commandment that says: When you love, love rightly. Love truly. Love without feigning it. Love when it hurts. Love with both body and soul. Love so it lasts.

This kind of love is beyond the body, beyond marriage, beyond simple friendship. It is love for the long haul, in season and out, with the soul far more than with the body. Which is why substituting another body for it never works.

And for you . . .

"Those are poor indeed," Thomas Fuller wrote, "who can promise nothing." The promise we make to another person to care for that person, to honor that person, to cherish that person demands as much sacrifice as it gives joy. When all we can promise is to stay in a relationship as long as the joy lasts, we have never been in a real relationship at all.

Don't be afraid to love, but by all means be afraid of confusing the impulses of the body with the instincts of the soul. If the spirits don't match, no responses of the body will make up for it.

Adultery is about a lack of focus. "Chains do not hold a marriage together," Simone Signoret wrote. "It is threads, hundreds of tiny threads, which sew people together through the years." It's weaving those threads that counts.

We say we love a lot of things — and then ignore them for the sake of something else. That's double-heartedness. It's a sign either of insincerity or of unconcern. In both cases, it has more to do with what's missing in ourselves than what's lacking in the other.

To love someone well, we have to get to know them without either tying them to ourselves or tying ourselves to them. That love is best that leaves both people free to be themselves.

When I don't allow the person I say I love to grow to full stature, that person has nothing to bring to the relationship. Then I will surely go looking for someone more interesting, more alive, more fun to be around.

Fidelity is the willingness to go on growing in a relationship that is based on mutual growth. "Marriage," Joseph Barth wrote, "is our last and best chance to grow up."

Commitment is the byproduct of communication. When the sharing stops, the relationship is in danger. "Married couples who love each other," the Chinese proverb teaches, "tell each other a thousand things without talking." If you know what your partner is thinking, respond to it. If you don't, ask yourself why.

Adultery happens. Sometimes it's a fancy; sometimes it's an affair. But it is always a call to change something. Ending the adultery does not save a relationship unless we take it as a warning to see what's really wrong.

Sometimes the "other person" is a job or a desired promotion or an obsession or a hobby. It's not always sex. And those things can be much more difficult to deal with than sex because that kind of immorality always feels so moral.

What brings a person back home again is not control; it's freedom. "Let there be spaces in your togetherness," Kahlil Gibran wrote. Why? Because when the other person is what completes me, it's distance that proves that. Then I always come back looking for it.

Relationships are not made out of service. They are made out of mutual respect. As Joe Murray puts it, "Marriage should be a duet — when one sings, the other claps." If the feelings are beginning to unravel between two people, they need to ask who isn't clapping.

Seventh

THE LAW OF SHARING

You shall not steal.

—Exodus 20:15

In the beginning...

Before deciding that "You shall not steal" is either clear in its meaning or unnecessary in its explanation or obvious in its application, consider two pieces of contemporary information. The first compares the wages U.S. corporations pay their chief executives with the amount paid to other CEOs around the world. In Germany, a corporation executive earns twenty-one times as much as the average worker; in Japan, sixteen.

In 1980, the CEOs of U.S. corporations received 42 times the wage of the average worker. By 1990, the ratio had risen to 85 times the pay of the average worker. In 2000, it was 531 times greater than the workers whose labors made their profits possible.

Or to put it another way, the United Nations Development Program reported in 1998 that the world's 225 richest people had a combined annual income equal to that of the world's 2.5 billion poorest people. That is approximately half the population of the globe. Sixty of those people live in the United States.

These are the people who insist that welfare programs must be cut and that tax breaks are needed to secure the profit margins of the wealthiest companies in the world.

In a world such as this, the seventh commandment, "You shall not steal," is as fresh as the morning paper. The Hebrew concept of stealing as it was heard by a nomadic, rural, pastoral clan was far different from the way we read it today. We presume that the function of criminal law is to protect the property of the rich from the greed of the poor. Israel, on the other hand, presumed that the function of this commandment was to protect the common property of the clan — the water well, the grazing land, the sheep — from being expropriated by the individual for the sake of personal profit.

To the Israelite, all property was owned in common and the welfare of the community superseded all individual appropriations. God owned the land; they were at best only its keepers, its caretakers, its stewards. It had been "loaned" to them for the welfare of all. To deprive any member of the community of their share, to deprive them of their needs, was to sin against God.

The concept is an ancient and a hallowed one, still alive and thriving in Native American tribes, whose lands we fenced off for our own designs in the Indian Wars of the nineteenth century, still residual in the design of those European towns where public grazing rights are still part and parcel of the town "commons."

Only when the Israelites began to settle in urban areas, in Canaanite towns, did the concept of private property and its security emerge as another dimension of the common life. To this day, the whole notion of "private" property and its relationship to the common good is a questionable one. Wealthy nations rob under-developed nations of their national resources, their labor, and their land at unconscionable prices.

Instead, Israel wrote laws, not to protect the rich from the poor but to protect the poor from being exploited by the rich. Scripture is replete with warnings against using false weights in the weighing out of grain in the market place, or charging interest on a debt, or holding the cloak of a debtor as collateral overnight even though he might die from exposure without it.

The laws of charity, of almsgiving, of distribution of goods are clear in Judaism. A minimum of one-tenth of one's income belongs to God and should be used to take care of God's people (Gen. 28:22). No Israelite could escape the obligation to care for those who could not care for themselves: the priests because they gave themselves entirely to the works of God and the poor because they were not able to support themselves.

Gleaning — the right of the poor to the ungathered part of the harvest in the field and the obligation of the farmer to leave part of the season's yield behind, even what drops from the farmers' carts at the end of the harvesting day — assured the poor of Israel their own portion of every harvest. Even the harvest they did not plant, did not tend, and did not gather.

The first-fruits of every yield belong to God, as well. The best — not the worst of what a farmer grew — belonged to those in need. Every Jew, even the poor, Hebrew law dictated, was expected to give at least one-third of a shekel per year to help those even poorer than they. There is no talk here of cutting back on welfare funds so that the rich can get richer.

The Bible forbids waste as certainly as it commands charity. "You must not destroy trees," Deuteronomy commands (Deut. 20:19). Nothing that is of use to anyone is ever to be destroyed and must be put to use for those who need it. To waste food, to give in to conspicuous consumption by throwing away something that still has value in order simply to get a new one, is stealing from those who have need of such things but can't possibly afford to get them for themselves.

The social implications of such a heritage stand to change the way a society operates. To have inner-city schools without computer labs while the children of the rich dispose of two and three computers a year violates what the Hebrews knew to be a commandment "not to steal." For corporations to use regular leasing plans on high-tech items that are discarded annually without distributing those things to groups that need them is, as far as the Bible is concerned, defrauding the poor.

Stealing, in the biblical sense, then, is not so much a private or personal sin as it is a social sin. To take what we do not need, to destroy what is useful to another, to deprive those in the community of their basic needs is stealing.

Strict honesty in business dealings is the foundation of the entire Torah, the Jew learns. It is, the Jewish child knows, the first thing for which a person is judged in the heavenly court. Business and a career are always to be considered secondary to our duties toward God, however successful the business, however consuming the career.

In the final analysis, then, this commandment cries out for us today to rethink the Western notion that the accumulation of wealth is an ideal worthy of a human life. It reminds us that sharing is the human imperative because we all depend on someone else somehow to provide what we each need. None of us is entirely self-sufficient. It warns us that compensation must be just. It reminds us that stealing is as much about method as it is about money.

In a world where credit card companies charge from 12 to 21 percent interest and 3 billion people are living on less than $2.00 a day while the average CEO of a Fortune 500 company is earning over $8,500,000 annually, "You shall not steal" may be the commandment that proves what Jesus meant when he said, "It is easier for a camel to pass through the eye of a needle, than for the rich to get into heaven" (Matt. 19:24).

The "deal," the "scam," the legal loopholes that form the business patterns of the twenty-first century make stealing the template, the foundation, of the business world. Those who have get more. No questions asked. But those who have nothing get only disdain.

With the rise of the middle class and the industrialization of the Western world, reformist theology swung away from the scriptural obligation to provide the poor with ways to glean their livelihood off the surplus of others. Instead, the whole philosophy of "rugged individualism" emerged. Those who could get could have. Those who could not get died in the gutters of the newly emerging cities or lived in squalor. They sold their bodies to the evils of day labor in the nineteenth century and felt their souls smothered by the shame of being dependent on handouts and bread lines in the twentieth century.

Now small checks, too slim to assure their dignity and reluctantly given, deprive their children of medical care and three meals a day.

Stealing has become the order of the day in a world bulging with wealth and teeming with the poor at the same time.

The interpretation of the commandment, shrunk to the level of the personal, gives a very specious comfort to those for whom the theme of social justice has long been missing in their understanding of the Decalogue's mandate for communal sharing. "You shall not steal" has been reduced to mean no shoplifting, no pilfering, no pickpockets, no burglary, no petty theft. It has become the province of poor people, sick people, immature people.

But the stealing the Decalogue really has in mind, is really concerned about, has actually become the sin of rich people, powerful people, people in a position to say "take it or leave it" to those who seek a living wage or subsidized housing or medical benefits and pensions.

"I have heard the cry of my people in Egypt" (Exod. 3:7), Yahweh says to Moses in the burning bush, "and I mean to deliver them." The awesome thought of Yahweh bringing down plagues on a people who treated them poorly, overworked and underpaid them, sends a tremor through the entire Hebrew scriptures. If we listen carefully, it is almost possible to feel the shudder again, now, in our own time, when 225 wealthy people have an annual income equal to that of 2.5 billion of the poorest people on the planet and, as a result, the poorest die daily from starvation.

And then ...

Stealing is not about things. Stealing is about relationships. And, if the daily paper is any kind of testimony to the quality of this society at all, ours are going to dust.

CNN ran a story recently that sent my mind spinning into space. High schools, the story reported, were now beginning to ban camera phones from classrooms. Why? Well, not because students are using cell phones in the halls. Not because they are typing crazy messages to one another during lectures. Not because they are playing games on them when they are supposed to be studying. Not because they are ringing during class. No, the school banned camera phones because a student in one class was caught photographing and mailing the test in front of him to a student somewhere else in the building. The scheme was a simple one. One student would mail the test; the other one would mail back the answers or use it to prepare to take the same test later in the day.

Stealing, it seems, has become high art in the United States.

Corporations do it with the pension funds of working people who have saved all their lives doing backbreaking labor only to discover years later that their funds have been looted by the very people who do not need pension money at all.

Presidents do it by siphoning off money from one project to another without submitting the transaction for the Congressional approval it requires.

Packagers do it by inflating the size of the product box and then charging more for it than the same item more modestly packaged that is sitting on the grocery shelf next to it.

Vendors do it by charging what the traffic will bear rather than what the item is worth.

And now we have the dawning notion that elections can be stolen, too, just by banning voters, losing ballot boxes, and programming computer voting machines.

Camera phones and computers weren't listed in the little book of sins they used to give to second graders when they were preparing them for First Communion. Then it was all about money: about finding money and failing to return it; about taking money out of your mother's purse without her permission; about eating things off the candy rack in the corner grocery store without paying for them.

It was nice, straightforward, "honest stealing."

Not now. Now honest stealing has become sneaky stealing. Worse, it has become big business. Now we take it for granted. That's the way things are, we say. Everybody does it, we say. It goes with the territory, we say.

Why? Well, Friedrich Schiller put it this way: "It is criminal to steal a purse. It is daring to steal a fortune. It is a mark of greatness to steal a crown. The blame diminishes as the guilt increases." "White-collar crime," we call it. And we blink with a kind of respectful amazement at the brilliance of it all. No wonder high school kids are inventing new ways of doing it. It's the "in thing." It's the smart way to get ahead. It's what you have to do to survive in a culture where stealing has become the mark of the truly successful. The sin now is not about the stealing; it's about getting caught.

It may be time to give the seventh commandment a lot more attention than we do — if, that is, we ever want to be able to trust one another again.

And for you...

How honest we are about little things determines eventually how straight we will be about the big ones — not simply in our own lives but in the society around us.

There is another kind of stealing we don't talk about. This kind involves having more than we need and giving nothing to those who don't have anything. This kind steals by consuming, controlling, hoarding all the goods of the earth for oneself. We call it "rugged individualism." Don't be fooled: it's spiritual gluttony.

Using up the goods of the earth, controlling the basic necessities of a society — land, housing, clothing, and food — takes from those who can't afford to buy what we have but also can't afford to do without it. Why else do some children begin to sell drugs if not to get what they can't get any other way.

Small-time thieves we put in jail. Why? For what purpose? To what end? "Prisons," Governor Jerry Brown said once, "don't rehabilitate, they don't punish, they don't protect, so what the hell do they do?" Now there's a question that begs to be answered in a society where jails are the only growth industry and in a nation whose schools are deteriorating.

The ancients know what we refuse to admit, it seems. The second-century Roman senator Marcus Aurelius wrote, "Poverty is the mother of crime." Until all people have access to basic necessities — food, housing, jobs, education, medical assistance, and sanitation — the people who take those things for granted will be prisoners of affluence. Posh affluence maybe, but prisoners nevertheless.

When we pilfer from another what we have not earned for ourselves, we gain a bit of property, perhaps, but we lose a lot of soul in the process.

"You shall not steal" really means, "You shall keep your integrity." When we cheat and steal we lose a great deal more of ourselves than we can possibly gain. We say poverty leads to stealing; the Iraqis say stealing leads to poverty. Think about it.

Stealing is stealing whether we are taking from the poor or taking from the rich. Overpricing a thing just because the population can pay for it is still stealing. It is also why the class system is maintained even when we say we don't have one.

Study your personal "financial report" and you will know your theology of life. What do you buy? To whom do you give? What don't you buy? To whom do you not give?

The things we choose to possess, the desires we have — satisfied or not — tell us who we really are. Down deep. In the very heart of us. No matter how it looks to others. "I'm not buying a car," said Canadian cartoonist Lynn Johnson. "I'm buying a lifestyle."

When life becomes, as it has in the United States, the limitless possession of things, stealing will naturally become a way of life. Only when we cultivate the dimensions of life that have something to do with life itself rather than with wealth can we ever become a truly honest people.

We cannot claim that we are not a nation of thieves until we insist on a society where no one has to steal to live. Anatole France put it this way: "The law, in its majestic equality, forbids rich and poor alike to sleep under bridges, beg in the streets or steal bread." Ouch.

Eighth

THE LAW OF SPEECH

You shall not bear false witness against your neighbor.
— Exodus 20:16

In the beginning...

One of the more disturbing pieces of moral data released in a while deals with the place of honesty in American culture. The Josephson Institute of Ethics has been surveying the ethics of American youth every other year since 1992. In 2002 the survey included twelve thousand high school students and found that almost 7 percent of them had cheated on a test. More than 33 percent said they'd stolen something from a store, and 93 percent said they'd lied to a parent, relative, or teacher. Most surprising of all, perhaps, was the fact that students at religious high schools were more likely to cheat and lie. In 2002, the cynicism factor — the notion that "a person has to lie or cheat sometimes in order to succeed" — jumped 9 percent to 43 percent.

What's more, as the study indicates, the numbers in every category are increasing substantially from year to year. The numbers bear watching. In years to come, they could have an impact on us all. "The scary thing," Michael Josephson, president of the Josephson Institute of Ethics, said, "is that so many kids are entering the work force to become corporate executives, politicians, airplane mechanics and nuclear inspectors with the dispositions and skills of cheaters and thieves." The thought of a corporate culture vitiated at its core by a total disregard for truth by the people who control it turns upside down the very lynchpin of our entire society. If we cannot trust one another to make honest contracts, to provide honest information, to function honestly in interpersonal relations, what can we trust about our society as a whole — its professionals, its bankers, its politicians?

The words are ominous. The questions they raise are even more troubling. How is it that a traditional regard for truth seems to be in danger? Perhaps the more important underlying question is, What are we teaching about the nature of "success" in this culture?

The answer may lie in the fact that the eighth commandment — "You shall not bear false witness against your neighbor" — has two historical dimensions to it. One of them we have learned to revere. The other we have failed, perhaps, to understand and to teach — both in its meaning to others and in its effect on ourselves.

The first level of witness, as the commandment implies, refers simply and directly to the legal system — to those who give "witness" in a court of law. In fact, such laws were common to all the major cultures of the Middle East.

The commandment, obviously, is not meant to be merely exhortatory. It deals with both important subject matter and issues of significant substance to the community. Peoples everywhere, it seems, recognized the need to protect the legal system itself from dishonesty and perversion.

To bring false witness against a person in a court of law is both a serious misuse of the judicial system and an attack on the accused whose reputation, if not his life, is at stake. Lying, people seemed to know instinctively, was no small thing.

Harsh attempts to assure the integrity of the legal system were basically universal as a result, and definitely not unique to the Torah. The Code of Hammurabi, for instance, hundreds of years before the Mosaic law, had already decreed that in the event a false accuser were unmasked in his malice, he (since only males could testify) was to receive the very punishment to which he had exposed the accused. To knowingly make a false accusation of murder — a capital crime — against an innocent person condemned the accuser himself to death.

This first level of "witness," a public one, demands a commitment to factual truth. But there is a second level of "false witness" that must be considered as well.

The second facet of the eighth commandment is far more subtle, far more troublesome than the first. The second aspect refers to speech as a sacred act. The insight astounds. In a world where false advertising is a given, where "hype" is some kind of clever exaggeration that is seldom confronted, commonly believed, speech has become anything but "sacred." In this culture, we are more likely to smile ruefully at those who are gullible enough to believe what they're told than we are to castigate, let alone convict, those making false claims. Saying only part of the truth or not saying the crucial part of the truth is all the same. Drug companies, tobacco companies, car companies, stockbrokers have become masters at it, in fact. We are at the point where getting away with the clever untruth is part of what it takes to be a success.

But it was not meant to be that way.

"If a man makes a vow to God, or makes an oath to obligate himself, he must not profane his word," the Book of Numbers teaches. He must not violate what makes a human, human and me, me. "Your speech betrays you," the poets say — and the poets are clearly correct. What I say defines me as a person as much as it defines what I'm talking about: it names me honest or dishonest, righteous or unrighteous, full of integrity or morally bankrupt of soul.

Speech is sacred because it is godlike. It creates our world. It gives new life or takes it. It promises and guarantees or it makes the world a harsh place to be. It builds trust and community or it destroys it. Indeed, speech makes us the type of person we are — true or false, godlike or not, co-creator or destroyer of the word that makes a people, a people.

To speak is to make a reality. To make a false one about anyone or anything is to profane the self, of course. But it also violates creation as God has made it by naming it something other than it is. It undermines the kind of trust the human community needs to function together as one family of God. It erodes personal relationships. It countermines the credibility of the self.

But lying does even more than that. Lying obscures the real self — even from the self. The more I begin to lie easily, facilely, even unnecessarily, the more the truth turns to putty in my mind. It gets harder and harder to know what truth is, what is really "true" in all the untruth. When I lie long enough, I lose touch with what I really think, really feel, really am. I simply no longer know myself whether what I say is what happened or what I want to have happened or what I'm afraid happened or what I want other people to believe happened. I am becoming a walking charade of dueling fantasies.

Lying reduces me to my own false self; it shrinks the most sacred part of me to the unholy; it violates the image of God in me.

But, the Torah is clear, all lies are not the same. Confusing one with the other and failing to point out the difference only creates other problems, other sins. There are sometimes two truths to be reckoned with in speech:

the truth of the situation on the one hand and, on the other hand, a different truth about the same situation. For instance, the Talmud (K'tubot 16b–17a) records an argument between the major theological schools of Hillel and Shammai on the subject. The Talmud reads: "How does one praise a bride while dancing before her at her wedding?

"The school of Shammai says: Describe the bride as she is.

"The school of Hillel says: Describe the bride as beautiful and full of grace.

"The school of Shammai retorted to the school of Hillel: But suppose she is lame or blind. Is one to say, 'O bride, full of grace,' seeing that scripture declares 'Keep away from anything false' (Exod. 23:7 in Mishpatim).

"The school of Hillel replied to the school of Shammai: In your opinion, if a person has made a bad purchase in the marketplace, should a friend praise it to his face or belittle it? Surely we should praise it to his face. Hence, the Sages inferred that we should always endeavor to be pleasant to other people."

The principle is clear: If no one gains unjustly by the lying, the "lie" does not "profane" us. We have a responsibility to keep private things private. We have a right not to expose ourselves to the world. The desire for privacy does not make our speech unholy. Nor does the intent to be kind make our speech untrue. On the contrary. As a friend of mine was fond of saying, "What is obviously not the truth is obviously not a lie."

But if someone gains unjustly by the lying, then we have besmirched creation, we have profaned the self.

If the moral content of culture is to be guaranteed, we must save the next generation from the false definitions of success that force them into cheating and lying in order to survive in it. We must teach them, as well, the difference between speech that is holy and the gossip, slander, calumny, and lying that destroy the very fabric of human community.

The eighth word of the Decalogue is honesty. It is the glue of the human race.

And then...

I had a Roman Catholic mother and a Presbyterian father. She taught me about the sacramental dimensions of life. He taught me to revere the truth. "Always tell the truth," he told me. "Never lie. It's not worth what it does to you when you're found out." It was a long time before I really understood that statement. Now I treasure it as one of the keys to having a real life.

I have come to understand, for instance, that stealing is one thing, but lying is another. Stealing takes from someone some thing that they have. Lying takes from people what they are: their reputation, their understanding, the quality of their lives. And the really interesting thing is that it takes those things from the one who lies as well as from the one who is lied about.

History is a record of life-stealing lies and their effects, even in the United States, and all of them meet the criteria: they not only affected the lives of others, they affected the public appreciation of the person themselves.

I remember where I was standing when Dwight D. Eisenhower, the avuncular, heroic president of the United States, confessed that he had lied to the American public about our use of spy planes over the sovereign territory of Russia. The presidency of the United States, the one thing an American could trust to the grave, turned within me to a pale shade of gray for the first time in my life. Eisenhower, a good man, had confessed within days of making the statement, but it was too late to save what had been an unblemished public life.

I know where I was when it was discovered that Richard Nixon's Watergate tapes had been erased. John Dean was proven true and another president, another piece of American integrity and dependability, disintegrated before our very eyes.

Lyndon Johnson lied about the Gulf of Tonkin. The Vietnamese didn't fire on us first as he had said in order to justify our invasion of Vietnam; we fired on them. The lie took us full-scale into a war that cost us 58,000 American lives, another 304,000 wounded, nine years of grief, and who knows now how many Vietnamese women, children, villages, rice paddies and grand-parents. And it cost Johnson the presidency as well.

Clinton lied about his personal life, and it cost him and us the pride we should have been able to savor in an otherwise great presidency.

Someone lied about the balloting and voting procedures in Florida in the presidential election of 2000 and left this country polarized, in turmoil, and left to deal with mistrust for four years. But it left the state of Florida itself cheapened and suspect in the eyes of the rest of the nation.

In every situation, the person who did the lying would have been better off telling the truth and the people who were lied to would have been quicker to forgive, surer about the future.

Lies go on in a way that stealing never does. People can recover with restitution. But lies blanket both the lied-about and the liars in suspicion, mistrust, and dishonor forever.

Even now, the whole country is struggling to determine where truth lies and what it means to all of us as citizens of the country, as citizens of the world. Were we really told the whole truth about why we invaded Iraq? And if not — whether we support the invasion or not — what does that say about us as a people?

And all of that is simply about politics. What about the lies that come out of economics? Or business practices? Or advertising? Or religion? What do those lies do — both to the institution itself and to the people affected by it?

"You shall not lie" is the spiritual mandate that is meant to save a great deal more than our reputations. It is a commandment meant to preserve an entire people from the cancer of mistrust, the individual from the pitfalls of pride, and the society from living with the corrosive effects of a culture of deceit.

And for you...

To be honest with another person is to respect that person's ability to deal with the truth. It is one of the highest compliments we can pay a person.

Lying is often an attempt to save another person from having to deal with a reality that they will, in the long run, have to face regardless. "Truth, like surgery," Han Suyin wrote, "may hurt, but it cures."

We lie, not simply about others, but even about ourselves. We put up false fronts and create fake realities about ourselves to impress others, to reassure ourselves of our own importance. "The most common lie," Nietzsche wrote, "is that in which one lies to himself; lying to others is relatively an exception."

107

What is the honesty quotient of the world we live in?
One thing we know for sure: it can only be as high as
our own.

When we ground ourselves in truth, we may be ostra-
cized for refusing to go along with the public lie, but
we cannot possibly be destroyed. "Truth," said Eliza-
beth Cady Stanton — who knew all there was to know
about being rejected for daring to speak a new truth —
"is the only safe ground to stand upon." I dare you.

When history is in the throes of change, as it is now,
every major institution will do everything it can to sup-
press the present, to hold on to the past, to maintain
old truths that are now new lies. "Honey in his mouth,"
the Chinese proverb reads, "knives in his heart." Then
goodness turns sour and that is the greatest falsehood
of them all.

The person telling the truth has the best memory. Lies
have multiple variations; truth but one.

Truth-telling is not high art. In fact, it's the easiest trick
of all. Samuel Butler said it this way: "Any fool," he
said, "can tell the truth, but it requires a person of some
sense to know how to lie well." The problem is that, in
the end, no one is that smart always.

If I myself am not honest, who can I possibly believe?

Lying is what makes us suspect in everything else in life.

It isn't that truth is rewarded; it is that truth needs no reward. Truth is its own reward: it requires no memory, no elaborate explanations, no conspiring confederates, and no fear of exposure.

When we lie about the other, it is the sign that there is something we do not like about ourselves. Something's missing. Something isn't right.

Ninth

THE LAW OF
SELF-CONTROL

You shall not covet your neighbor's wife.

—Exodus 20:17

In the beginning...

Jimmy Carter admitted to a reporter once that yes, there had been times in life that he had looked with interest at women other than his wife. He had "lusted after them in his heart," he said. He had never acted on those interests, he explained. But he was human. The thoughts came sometimes.

Some people responded with horror at the very thought of it. Other people argued that the statement had played into his lost election attempt. Where I came from, people simply laughed at the whole issue. "After all, what's the problem?" they asked.

And that is a very important question.

At first glance, the ninth and tenth commandments seem to be totally without substance, totally without value. In fact, how can they be "commandments" at all. After all, who can see "covetousness" — and anyway how many people would be as honest about it as Jimmy Carter? More to the point, in the end, who cares about it? After all, since when did wanting something have any moral importance as long as we don't do anything immoral in the process of getting it?

The problem is that it is that very line of reasoning which may simply indicate how really legalistic, how basically underdeveloped we are spiritually.

To begin to understand the connection between legalism and a lack of moral maturity, there are two things that need to be considered before it's possible to determine when a concern not to "covet" things is important or not. One seems basically unimportant. The second seems irrelevant.

In the first place, some groups count the commandments differently than others do.

Jewish law — and most of mainline Protestantism — treats as one and the same command what Roman Catholics and Lutherans call the ninth and tenth commandments. You shall not covet either the neighbor's wife or the neighbor's property.

In the same way, the Jewish tradition, unlike Catholic and Lutheran texts, treats "I, the Lord, am your God" and "You shall not have other gods besides me" as two separate commands. The first, Judaism teaches, recognizes the Oneness, the monotheistic character, of God. The second statement, Judaism insists, forbids the making of material images of God as if God can be "embodied," pinned down, identified as a white male, for instance.

Catholics and Lutherans — some say because both of those groups were partial to the use of images — conflated what Judaism called two separate commands into one to read: "I, the Lord, am your God, you shall not have other gods besides me." They saw them as two dimensions of the same mandate. The problem became that to have ten commandments they now had to present the interdiction against covetousness as two separate items.

The point is that though the ninth and tenth commandments treat of two different areas of life — of lust and greed — they both speak, at base, of "covetousness," of wanting what we should not, cannot, have.

It is covetousness that is at issue. Not sexual behavior, not acquisition. It is covetousness that is the problem. And it is covetousness, as a result, whose meaning and danger we are inclined to overlook in our emphasis on either sexual excess or the desire for wealth. It is not, in other words, "lusting in your heart." It is failing to be satisfied.

Covetousness is the spiritual disease of unbridled desire. It is the need to be satiated — and then to have even more. It is the need for constant satisfaction of the senses. It is the inability to be at peace with the self, with life, with necessities. It is self-aggrandizement gone mad and life gone totally narcissistic.

Covetousness is a sin of the soul, a sickness of the mind that leads to perpetual discontent. It is a hot prod in the center of the heart, always rousing us to want more than is necessary, always demanding that we find some way to get more than is possible, always pressing us to get what we want any way we can — whether we should have it or not.

Competition and comparison are the engines that drive otherwise healthy people to the pit of covetousness where only restlessness and dissatisfaction dwell. Nothing is ever good enough in this part of the soul. No amount of anything is ever enough. The unremitting effort to get more and more of everything we see becomes the standard of life that destroys us physically, eats our hearts out emotionally, and dries us to the core spiritually.

Competition for things pits us against the rest of the world and in the end forever leaves us losers. We lose to those who are stronger, smarter, wealthier, and better connected — however smart, strong, rich, or qualified we may be. There is always someone out there who is more so. Then covetousness — that raw, ruthless need to have what I want, get everything I can, outdo everyone I meet — consumes me and leaves me raging and restive once more.

Then everyone I meet is my potential enemy rather than a possible ally. They all stand there in plain sight threatening to humiliate me, to show me up, to put me in my place, to stop me from getting what I demand, to strip me of all the things I have so greedily gathered to hide the real me behind the me I am pretending to be.

I am left with nothing else to do but to compare myself to everyone around me, to run feverishly through life — trying to catch up, trying to win, trying to amass outside myself what I do not have within me: peace, satisfaction, a sense of wholeness.

If we can't see "covetousness," how is it that we can be mandated not to do it? And if it is an attitude of mind, not an action, how can it be a sin? What "word" is this to the people of God about the kind of life the one who purports to live a godly life is meant to model?

Actually, it may be the most important word of all: the word here is not simply praise or humility, worship or honor, care or fidelity, justice or honesty. The word that rings through the ninth commandment is the highest compliment that can be paid to a human being. The word is "control." We who are, the psalmist says, "little less than gods, little lower than the angels," have already what the rest of the cosmos lacks: the ability to control ourselves. It is the lack of control that is sinful. It is the substitution of baseless desire for reason, for will power, that is our greatest sin.

The power to choose for more than things, for more than satiation, is the glory of God in us. The ability to say no to ourselves is the crowning glory of being human.

This whole culture is ranged against that, of course. We are all told constantly what we must have to be noticed, what we must buy to be up-to-date, what we must wear to be successful, what we must do if we want to be seen as sophisticated, what we must be if we hope to become influential. But the ninth commandment is clear. We don't have to do any of those things. We do not need to feed the beasts of "desire and accumulation" who will own our souls and drive our minds mad with wanting.

Therein lies the power of the ninth commandment. It comes to stop us before we give way to the lust that not only sullies the body but also sours the soul. And Jimmy Carter, who confessed to having known lust in his heart, had also learned to say no to it.

And then...

Of all the commandments that are ignored, overlooked, or considered least useful, the ninth may rank most meaningless of all. Ironically enough, in this day and age, in this society, it may be most needed.

The problem is that most people miss the meaning of the ninth commandment entirely. They fail to realize that the very phrasing of the ninth commandment is a lesson in culture, in history, in society, and in human relations as well as in ongoing moral development.

This commandment, more than most, indicates how even our understanding of the moral life changes with time.

The original statement of the ninth commandment, for instance, reads "Thou shalt not covet thy neighbor's wife." Period. Wife. Not "Thou shalt not covet thy neighbor's husband," not "Thou shalt not covet thy neighbor's spouse." This commandment in its original intent only deals with the injustice of one man's taking another man's property. This commandment is about male property rights. It is not really about the sanctity, the power, the inviolability of the marital relationship.

In those days, women, like land and animals, belonged to men. Fathers gave their daughters away to another man in marriage; mothers did not give their sons away to another woman. Men did not belong to women. Nor could women own anything at all. They had no property rights, no financial independence, no legal identity, no rights before the courts.

For centuries, men could, and usually did, have multiple wives. Women, on the other hand, were allowed to have only one husband. The situation was very clear about who owned whom. In some parts of the world, to this day, the situation has yet to change.

But, at least for some parts of the world, we have come to translate the statement to mean something very different, to talk about what it means to destroy the bonds that make a pair a couple, a relationship, a home.

The problem is that in the broadening of the interpretation — important as it is, good as it is, significant as it is, we are at the point that we now risk misunderstanding another undercurrent of this commandment that may be more important than ever in our society.

This commandment is about lust, about the insatiable need not simply to have more than we need but to have more than is good for us.

This commandment is about the degradation that comes with trying to suck all the air out of life and so failing to be satisfied with anything.

Lust is the attempt to consume everything we see. Lust also means that what we see consumes us as well.

Pornography is lust. The sexual exploitation of women and men is lust. The division of people into types — some expendable, some not — is lust. The hiring of women at lesser pay than men to do the same job the man does is lust. The "downsizing" of an older man just before his pension comes due is lust. The hiring of younger people rather than experienced people so we can get their energy without paying for their experience is lust.

"Thou shalt not covet the body of thy neighbor's spouse" is a commandment we could all stand to visit again in this lustful age of ours.

And for you...

When we use another person's body for our own satisfaction in any way whatsoever, sexually or commercially, rather than for that person's good as well as our own, that's lust — with or without the sex.

When men are really men, women don't need to be protected.

When we want what is not ours we want what, in the end, will possess us more than we possess it.

The use of others begins slowly and then, over time, becomes the habit that not only dehumanizes the other; it dehumanizes ourselves as well.

Lust is not really about sex; it is about desire. It is not about pleasure; it is about power. It is not about love; it's about control.

"Women must learn not to be subservient to the wishes of their fathers, husbands and partners," Petra Kelly wrote, "because then they do not fulfill their own ambitions." Only love that is free to come and go, to become the fullness of itself, is really love at all.

Lust is the seat of dissatisfaction, not satisfaction, because it keeps us perpetually unhappy with what we have.

Don't worry about what you don't get in life; worry about what you do get. The way we deal with what we have determines the way we deal with everything else around us. It also measures the quality of our souls.

When we pursue a person for the physical release they promise us rather than for the spiritual growth they require of us, we have sold our souls to the quest of the ephemeral, the unreal, and the totally temporary.

"There are two great tragedies in life," George Bernard Shaw wrote. "One is not to get your heart's desire. The other is to get it." Desire keeps us going. Lust stops us in our tracks by pretending to give us what we need but then we discover that it only leaves us empty again.

John Lahr, the American critic, said, "Society drives people crazy with lust and calls it advertising." We are a culture, in other words, that cultivates lust — the desire for what we do not own and do not need and cannot contain — and then wonders why so many people are unhappy in life.

The Buddha taught that "Just as a tree, though cut down, can grow again and again if its roots are undamaged and strong, in the same way if the roots of craving are not wholly uprooted sorrows will come again and again." It isn't what we have that makes us unhappy; it's what we want that leaves us dull to the present, unaware of what we have.

Tenth

THE LAW OF ASSURANCE

You shall not covet your neighbor's goods.

—Exodus 20:17

In the beginning...

Among all the stories in ancient monastic folklore, one stands out as a particularly insightful commentary on the tenth commandment. Once upon a time, the story teaches, a disciple traveled for miles to sit at the feet of an old nun who had acquired an unusual reputation for holiness. People came from far and wide simply to watch her work, to listen to her chant, to hear her comment on the scriptures. Here without doubt was a person of substance, an impacting personality, an imposing figure.

What the seeker found when he finally reached the site of her hermitage, however, was only a tiny little woman sitting on the floor of a bare room plaiting straw baskets alone.

Shocked, the seeker said, "Old woman, where are your books? Where are your chair and footstool? Where are your bed and mattress?"

And the old woman answered him back, "And where are yours?"

"But I'm only passing through," the seeker said.

"And so am I," said the old woman knowingly.

At first glance, the final instruction of the Ten Commandments, "Thou shalt not crave things" — an alternate translation of the ninth and tenth words of the Decalogue — seems to be a strange insertion into a document designed to create a new kind of human community. It also seems to be a vacuous one.

Is this concern about yearning for things really the ultimate summit, the peak moment, the most profound insight, the crowning glory, the culminating insight into which the law is meant to lead us? The whole sorry implication of ending the Decalogue, life-changing rules of order, with an anemic little article like this one recalls T. S. Eliot's comment on life when he says, "This is the way the world ends, this is the way the world ends . . . not with a bang but a whimper."

You shall not crave things, you shall not covet, hardly seems like the final chord in a document that formed a people and created an ethic that gave character to the entire Western world.

But the inability to think beyond the obvious about this culminating word of the Decalogue may simply be the sign that we ourselves have not yet come to see beyond things or to live for more than wanting. It may mean that the commandments are yet in the process of coming to fullness in us.

Scholars argue from generation to generation about whether or not the commandments are more action centered than idea centered, more concerned with ethical behavior or with the development of right attitudes. The ninth and tenth commandments are particularly problematic. How can they be simply about wanting things, commentators argue, when all the other commandments — except the first — specify particular behaviors: take responsibility for your own actions, keep the Sabbath, take care of the elderly, don't kill people, don't violate them, don't steal from them, don't lie to them? The problem is clear: unless these last two commandments are also about actions, unless they mean something like "don't plot evil" rather than simply "don't want what you can't have," Why are they here? What is their use?

The answer emerges clearly in every ancient spiritual tradition, in every experience of the human pursuit of the divine in life. Spiritual masters in every generation of every people in every great tradition acknowledge the awareness that only God is everything. Only God is really enough. Only when we see beyond all the things in which we are immersed, only when we learn to hold them all with a relaxed grasp, can we ever discover the One in whom all of them take their being.

To the Hindu, the process is made plain in the *sanyasi,* the seeker who leaves all things — life, career, family — to seek the God within.

In Buddhism, the purpose of life is to achieve nirvana, the state of desirelessness in which all suffering disappears and the seeker sinks into the flow of the universe without expectations, without demands.

In Islam it is the witness of the Sufi, who remind us that there is a life above what we call life in which creature and creator come to one heart, one mind, even now, even here.

In Israel, I believe, it is in the culminating insight that comes from faithful adherence to the ninth and tenth commandments, the realization that the mystical awareness of the One God to which the first commandment leads us is everything, is enough, is all there is, is what life is really about. In Christianity the mystical tradition developed what the Decalogue implies: if you put down your desires for everything other than God, the mystics teach, you will find God. Beyond accumulation and possessiveness, the One to whom the entire Decalogue points will take hold of you and capture you completely.

In Judaism, Moses entered "the dark cloud where God was" (Exod. 20:21). It is this experience to which we are all invited in the living of the Decalogue. What the ninth and tenth words of the Decalogue call us to is what every major religious tradition identifies as an essential of the spiritual life. It is the separation of the self from the purely material aspects of life so that we can come to know the spiritual.

Detachment, that movement away from being possessed by particular things in order to make room in ourselves to be possessed by God, is not the deprivation of things. It is the emptiness that possesses the Everything there is in life of lasting value.

At that moment, at the moment of genuine detachment, the great mystical traditions say to us, we come to the core of the spiritual life — a core that is beyond behavior, beyond laws, beyond the simple ethics of the spiritual life to the point in which we find God in everything and everything in God.

The first commandment, "I, the Lord, am your God, you shall not have other gods besides me," whether the beginner in the spiritual life realizes it or not, encompasses all the other commandments. In them, through them, we move beyond all the false gods of life that seek to entrap us.

We go beyond the search for a magical God who will curse whom we want cursed. We find our way through the shrines we build to our own egos to praise the life above all other life. We learn to care for those before us and the wisdom they bring into our lives. We come to value and protect the lives of others. We begin to reverence intimacy rather than denigrate sex. We refuse to enrich ourselves by impoverishing the other.

We learn to use truth to bring life, not death, to those around us.

Then, finally, we are ready to put down our attachment to any of these things — to the persons or property we use so cavalierly, amass so arrogantly, pursue so lewdly — that bolster our narcissism and feed the false god that is our self.

Then we have the new community. Then we have a new kind of people. Then we have a sign of the Oneness, the Greatness, the Allness of God. Then "I, the Lord, am your God, you shall not have other gods besides me" — the very essence of the Decalogue, the foundation of a new and healthy life — is complete.

We are free now of the compulsions that drive us. We are healthy again in mind. We cease to be driven by unrealizable and bogus needs. We do not need to compete. We cease to compare ourselves to others. We do not need to buy the bigger ring, the faster car, the larger house, the finer clothes, the more expensive wine anymore. We can simply be ourselves — full of life, full of peace, full of God.

Then shalom finally comes. We are at peace — with ourselves, with our neighbors, with our God.

The essence of the ninth and tenth commandments is, in the end, really the substance, the embodiment of the first commandment: It is the putting away of idols, the melting into God, the awareness that there is only one thing in life that matters. Finally.

And then . . .

I heard a story a long time ago that helped me to understand three things: the daily newspaper, the tenth commandment, and the difference between most lives and some lives.

The story tells of an exhausted American business-man who traveled to a faraway island for a vacation. Every day he went to the beach to swim, and every day he found a native there slowly cleaning fish in his boat.

"Do you catch fish every day?" the visitor asked. "Oh, yes," the native said. "Plenty fish here." "Well," the visitor asked, "how often do you fish?" "I fish every morning," the native said.

"But what do you do then?" the businessman asked. "Well," the native said, "first I clean the fish for supper, then I take a little siesta, then I build a bit of my house, then I eat with my family, and then, for the rest of the night, I play my guitar, visit with my friends, and drink my homemade wine."

"But don't you see?" the visitor asked. "If you fished all day, you could sell your fish, buy a bigger boat, hire helpers, can, pack, and sell your fish all over the world, and make a lot of money."

"But what would I do with it?" the native replied.

"Why, you could buy a house, quit working, enjoy your family, take big vacations, and party with your friends for the rest of your life!"

"Mister," the native said to the businessman, "that's what I'm doing now and I only have to catch one fish a day to do it."

"You shall not covet your neighbor's goods," the tenth commandment teaches, and like the old native, the tenth commandment knows what it's talking about. It's warning us about the gnawing, groaning, smothering effects of greed on the human soul. It's talking about dooming ourselves to the spiritual disease of "perpetual dissatisfaction."

Every day our newspapers demonstrate the effects of it: Billionaires cheat to get more money. Businesses cheat customers and workers and one another to make greater profits. Governments collude with other governments to cheat their own people out of wages and workers' benefits for the sake of the personal payoffs that come to those who choose graft over just gains.

And for what? For the very same things that average hardworking people get all the time: a house, a car, a family, a few good friends, decent food, an education, a social life. Nothing else. The same things, all priced to provide what the traffic can afford. Cotton sheets or silk sheets, a resort or a cabin in the woods, perch or lobster, wood or vinyl interiors. Depending.

When you come right down to it, at the end of the day there's not all that much different in the things to be gotten by money at either end of the financial spectrum, except to get more of them. A TV in every room that nobody watches, a car collection, the same kind of condo in the same kind of places, most of them empty all of the time. And people everywhere to pay for taking care of them.

"Those who have cattle have care," the Kenyans say. But remember, God said it first.

Most of us have everything we need. Greed is the compulsion to get more because we refuse to enjoy what we have.

My advice? Remember the native fisherman.

And for you...

Perhaps one of the greatest philanthropists of modern times, John D. Rockefeller, understood the difference between greed and gain best. He said, "I know of nothing more despicable and pathetic than a person who devotes all the hours of the waking day to the making of money for money's sake." It is not wealth, in other words, that is in question. It is why we make it and what we do with it when we have it that makes the difference.

The compulsive need to amass things may be nothing more than a signal of the emptiness of our souls.

To work hard, to play well, to enjoy life, to give to others, and to be satisfied with what we have may be the only criteria we need to know whether or not we have really succeeded in life.

In this culture a sense of "enoughness" is a sign of mental aberration. A need for "moreness" is considered normal. What a pathetic way to go through life, always grasping, always greedy — always discontented with the self.

Greed can lead to jealousy, which means that I not only never get enough of the things I want but the more things I see, the more friends I lose. "Whenever a friend succeeds," Gore Vidal wrote, "a little something in me dies." Pitiable. Truly pitiable.

To cure greed we must learn to love something enough to be willing to do without everything else but it.

If you want to break the tendency to greed, when you get something new, unless you go on using the first one as well as the second one, try giving the old one away. If you find yourself simply storing it, beware.

If the Northern Hemisphere is unduly rich, it can only be because the Southern Hemisphere is unduly poor. "International business may conduct its operations with scraps of paper," Eric Ambler wrote, "but the ink it uses is human blood." What we do as a people to other peoples of the world will surely come back on our own heads. If for no other reason than that one, that's why international law is everyone's concern.

Beware what you value in life. You may get exactly what you're looking for without any of the cure for it. Or as Imelda Marcos said once with great indignation: "I did not have 3,000 pairs of shoes; I had 1,060."

I know that Imelda Marcos had at least a thousand pairs of shoes because I saw them with my own eyes. But all I could think of when I looked at them was that if she wore one pair a day, every day of the year, each pair would be worn, on average, no more than once every three years. Or from twenty-five to thirty times in a person's entire life. Outside the palace, though, children walked through the streets wearing no shoes at all. That's not a hobby; that's greed. The question, I knew, was what is it in my life that is the equivalent of Imelda Marcos's shoes?

Greed eats away at the soul, distracts us from friendship, consumes us with want. "There is," the Buddha says, "no fire like passion, there is no shark like hatred, there is no snare like folly, there is no torrent like greed."

It isn't that greed is a sin against others that is its only evil. It is that greed is self-destructive that makes it so pathetic. Greed eats out the center of our own lives. We exhaust ourselves with envy instead of learning to enjoy what we already have.

Give one thing away every day for a month. It's called oiling the soul so it works better.

First Great Commandment

THE FIRST LAW OF LOVE

You shall love your God with all your heart and with all your soul and with all your mind.

—Matthew 22:36–37

In the beginning...

According to the Christian scriptures, Jesus himself gave this command to "love the Lord your God with all your heart." The question is, Where did he get it? Is it unique to us?

Love, Christians are fond of saying, is what distinguishes the Christian scriptures from the Hebrew scriptures. But the truth of the matter far exceeds the readiness of the assertion. There is no doubt that "love" is the determining value in all of Christian tradition. Love for the other becomes the standard Christianity sets for itself. On its presence or absence from Christian history, all of Christian history either rises or falls.

133

Christians are measured by it in century after century, sometimes found astonishingly true to its criteria, but too often found astonishingly lacking as well.

"See how they love one another" — the response of non-Christians to early followers of Christ, to those Christians down through the ages who ministered to slaves and lepers, the ill and the poor — became far too often the horror of the Crusades, the slaughter of Muslims, the Inquisition, the forced conversion of Native Americans, the oppression of women.

Love is the banner under which the Christian walks, yes. "Love your neighbor...love your enemies," Jesus said. "Little children, love one another," John said over and over again. "And the greatest of these is love," Paul writes in Corinthians. But Christians did not invent the religious or spiritual imperative to love.

"You shall love your neighbor as yourself," God demands of the Chosen People (Lev. 19:18). "You shall love the alien" (Lev. 19:34). "You shall love the stranger," the scripture goes on (Deut. 10:19). "Love intelligent slaves" (Sir. 7:21). "Love your friends" (Sir. 27:17). And you shall love the Lord your God with your whole heart, Deuteronomy says. The message seems clear. The law is not about law at all. It is about love.

But what does a disquisition on love have to do with the Ten Commandments themselves?

Why even talk about the Two Great Commandments? Why add commandments to the commandments. Aren't the Ten Commandments enough? The answer: Only if we understand that the commandments are about more than commandments. Only if we realize that the commandments are not about restrictions. They are about the things that make us whole. They are about the will of a loving God that the love that sustains the universe should never die.

Each element of the law requires us to love. Every dimension of every commandment deals with the justice that is the foundation of love. But Christians often fail to realize that law and love are two sides of the same reality. Law teaches the seeker how to love and so the love of the Creator demands the giving of the law. The only way the Jew knows for sure to "love the Lord" is to live the law given by a loving God.

The problem is that there is not just one version of the Ten Commandments in scripture. As a result, Christians are inclined to read the Hebrew scriptures as an exercise in law rather than love. And small wonder, perhaps.

Repetition itself seems to define the legalistic character of the Hebrew scriptures. There are several and various versions, for instance, all of them essentially the same in subject matter but none of them identical. Beyond that are the laws that are meant to explicate the Ten Commandments themselves. As a result, the law the psalmist praises for "showing us the path of life" is in Exodus, and the Book of Numbers, and Deuteronomy and Leviticus. It is no small body of law. And all of it is just slightly different everywhere.

Sometimes the differences lie in the selection of Hebrew words chosen to express or explain the same topic. When a Jew asks the question, What does it mean to love the Lord your God? the answer appears to come back in several forms. In the fifth commandment, we know, scholars struggle to this day to determine whether the command means "You shall not *murder*" or "You shall not *kill.*" The two meanings are a world apart. They make all the difference between whether or not we are called to be a law-abiding community or a loving pacifist community. And yet, at the same time, the commandment is clearly about the value of loving life, however you translate it.

Sometimes the difference between versions has to do with the way the content itself is treated. In the first rendering of the law, slaves are to be freed after six years of service. In the second, the slave and his whole family are to be released from servitude in the seventh year. Clearly, slaves are people, family counts, and the way we love those who are less powerful than we are has something to do with our own blessedness.

Then, too, whatever the actual statements themselves, scripture demonstrates that laws — concerning punishment, theft, slavery, even worship, for instance — changed from year to year, from situation to situation.

The implication to be drawn from such a history is an important one: Law grows. Law changes. Or, to put it another way, we grow in love. We change the way we need to love. We broaden in our understandings of life and relationships and human community and justice.

So are the Ten Commandments and all their elaborations in scripture obsolete, without meaning, inconsistent, and so vitiated at their very base? Hardly. What we learn about law here, about love here, is more important than any single law can ever be. We learn that law is simply a guide to a greater good, a basic good, love as a fundamental of life, a demonstration of the love of God.

We come to understand that principles are more important than particulars.

That in itself has something to do with the way we go about being a loving people rather than simply a legalistic one.

It is when we teach law as inflexible, rigid, and absolute that the law is destroyed, that the love that impels it shrivels. The function of law, the maintenance of order and justice, is about care. It's about a love affair with life. Laws that cannot change with circumstances assure us of neither law nor order. If anything, they do exactly the opposite. And most of all, they destroy love.

It is not the behaviors we require or proscribe under each commandment that counts. It is the intention of the commandment that counts.

When Moses came down from the mountain, scripture says, he came with two tablets of law. On the first tablet, the sages teach, were the first four commandments. On the second were the last six.

The first tablet, the rabbis taught, had to do with our relationship to God as supreme, all holy, worthy of worship, and co-creator with us of the human race. As that God loves us like a parent — "I carry them close to my heart as a nurse carries an infant..." (Num. 11:12) — so must we love and nurture the life we ourselves create.

It is that total, unadulterated consciousness of the love of God for us and our obligation, since we are made "in the same image," to love back in the same way — freely, fully, faithfully — that the first great commandment enshrines for us.

You shall love your God with all your heart and with all your soul and with all your mind, the first great commandment teaches. We are to do it, of course, by recognizing the One God, by never mocking that God, by worshiping that God, and by participating with that God in the glory of creation. But we are to do it more than mechanically or legalistically, more than simply by attending worship services, being careful not to swear, making sure that we make nothing else in life god but God. On the contrary, we are to do it totally.

To "keep" any of the commandments and forget God's love for us and our love for God is not to keep the commandments at all. It is simply to keep the law. And that is a paltry thing indeed.

And then...

One day a seeker approached Rabbi Hillel, one of Judaism's greatest teachers. "If you can teach me your whole religion standing on one leg," the seeker said, "I will become your disciple." And Rabbi Hillel answered him, "You shall love your God with your whole mind and your whole heart and your whole soul. Everything else is commentary."

Jesus, too, answered those who asked him what was the greatest commandment, "The greatest commandment is this: You shall love your God with your whole heart and your whole mind and your whole soul."

To study the commandments and miss this lesson is to miss the commandments entirely. The commandments do not measure our love of God; they only give it substance. They only ground it. They only demonstrate a desire to make it real.

We are accustomed, legalists that we are, however, to define a manual of sins for ourselves, a checklist of behaviors by which we measure our sanctity against the sanctity of those around us. The list is a comforting one. It allows us to feel holy without ever really having to be holy. It enables us to consider ourselves righteous without living rightly. It teases us into doing all the right things for the wrong reason.

It is more than possible to defer to authority, to go to church, to profess faith in God, to live a rigidly pure and loveless life, never to steal a penny, never to tell a

lie, never to give in to greed, never to succumb to lust —
and not really love God at all. "The worst treason," the
poet T. S. Eliot says, "is to do the right thing for the
wrong reason."

It's only when all the dimensions of our lives are lived
in accordance with a consciousness of God — when we
make nothing but God, god; when we put our hope,
not in money or things or people or power, but in God
alone; when we bow our souls before the omnipresent
presence of God in our lives — that the rest of the
commandments take on any real meaning in life at all.
Otherwise, why not cheat and steal and lie and rape and
plunder and horde? Why not make myself God?

We are inclined to forget that the commandments as
we know them are simply guidelines meant to show us
how to keep the greatest commandment of all — the
love of God — when the truth is that when we really
love God, we don't need any of the other commandments at all. A sense of the presence of God is more
than enough to guide us.

And for you...

The awareness that God is, and that I am accountable
to God, is the soul's greatest defense against arrogance
and the oppression of others. It's not possible to really
believe in the God of all and do evil to the other.

Real love of God takes possession of our hearts, gives direction to our souls, makes us channels of the ongoing energy of creation. "A desire to kneel down sometimes pulses through my body," Etty Hillesum wrote in a Nazi concentration camp. "It is as if my body had been meant and made for the act of kneeling."

A constant awareness of God connects us to the totality of the universe. It raises us above and beyond our tiny little selves to become part of the heartbeat of the universe. It gives life meaning and light.

The consciousness of God is what saves us from feeling alone in the cosmos. Otherwise we come and disappear, are born and go to dust—and all for nothing.

In each of us there is a memory of God. "We are not human beings trying to be spiritual," Jacquelyn Small wrote. "We are spiritual beings trying to be human." The memory of God that beats within us is the only hope we have that our very humanity is not what will distract us from the reason for our existence.

When we love God with our whole soul, there is nothing on earth that can possibly destroy our spirit or confuse our direction. Or as Charles Swindoll put it, "It helps me if I remember that God is in charge of my day—not I."

Everything I need to remind me that the purpose of my life is to melt into God — not to train God to do tricks for me — lies in the eternal rhythm of birth and death. I came into this life helpless and dependent, and I will leave it the same way. In between those two poles of humanity, my only task is to realize that the purpose of every step is simply to take me closer into God.

To live well, we must consciously reflect on the meaning of every facet of our lives. We must ask why we are doing a thing, why we don't do something else, what of the spirit is this moment meant to give us, where is God in this for us now? "I cannot walk an inch," Anne Sexton writes, "without trying to walk to God."

St. Augustine wrote: "We do not walk to God with the feet of our body, nor would wings, if we had them, carry us there. But we go to God by the affections of our soul." It's love of God, consciousness of God, awareness of God in the least godly thing that is union with God. When all of life is permeated with such recognition, life is complete.

To love God with our whole hearts and minds and souls means to place nothing above the final achievement of pure trust in the Mystery of life. "God does not die," Dag Hammarskjöld wrote, "on the day when we cease to believe in a personal deity, but we die on the day when our lives cease to be illuminated by the steady radiance, renewed daily, of a wonder, the source of which is beyond all reason."

Don't confuse "reason" with love. "Reason" is nothing but calculated speculation that God is. Love in the face of despair, love — even when there is apparently nothing in a situation to love — is sure proof that we are held in the grip of a magnet larger even than life itself.

As long as we think of God as only outside of ourselves rather than within us as well, we will never really be sure that God is the very air we breathe, the very heartbeat on which we are carried. Then we can forget God, miss God, overlook God, fail to find God. But when we know that God is all that keeps us alive, then we know God. As Meher Baba said, "The finding of God is the coming to one's own self."

Second Great Commandment

THE SECOND LAW OF LOVE

You shall love your neighbor as yourself.
—Matthew 22:39

In the beginning...

When Moses came down from Sinai carrying two tablets, the message was clear: the whole law does not lie in either aspect of it. To worship God without caring for the life that God created in the other is to attempt to separate the God of creation from the creation itself. Nonsense.

To attempt such a thing is to make a God out of religion and so fail to be really religious at the same time.

Scholars disagree about the dates and times, the circumstances and population of peoples in the exodus from Egypt. They disagree, too, about the time and place of the Sinai event. Was Aaron really there at all? Was Joshua in the same story or another story that later

144

gets conflated with the Moses story? But none of that is the point — any more than being able to document the story of Romulus and Remus in Rome, or the writing of the Vedas in India. They all have something to do with great cultural beginnings. They all say something about a people's awareness of itself. What the Ten Commandments do for us is far and beyond the historical niceties of their origin.

The point is that the scripture gives us — in the story of Sinai, in the nature of the Ten Commandments, in the Decalogue that became the foundation of a new way of life — a metaphor of human development. And human development is one of this culture's highest goals. People everywhere take emotional literacy classes. They go to personal development workshops. They go into psychoanalysis for years.

All of these things make for laudable exercises in the fine art of growing up, of being full human beings, of being healthy in mind as well as in body. At the same time, though all of them explore what it is in us that blocks a feeling of achievement, of goodness, of happiness, of success, none of them treat the spiritual dimensions of all those things.

The Ten Commandments do that.

What is it to "achieve" if we achieve less than we should as human beings? What is goodness of life if it leaves out the rest of life, leaves out everything but ourselves, in the equation? What is happiness if it depends on what we have and what we get when we never get what we think we should have? What exactly is "success" in life when everything we define it as now — social status, power, money, property — becomes useless to us in the end?

Then the Ten Commandments become a metaphor for human development, a chart by which we can measure our own spiritual development and with it, then, our personal growth.

It is the issues dealt with in the Ten Commandments that tell us what it is to be a full human being.

On the first set of Sinai Tablets, commandments one through four, the issue is creaturehood. These commandments demand that we come to grips with pride, with our place in the universe. To know the One God, the creator of the universe, is to know, indeed, that we are dust in the hourglass of eternity. We come to the kind of humility that makes it possible for us to listen and learn from the world around us.

The second commandment makes us deal with the desire in us for a magic kind of God who does for us what we ought to be making the effort to do for ourselves. We take God's name "in vain" when we expect God to save us from the wars we start or the bombs we build or the poverty we create.

The third commandment brings us to praise the God who gave us the law that leads us to wholeness.

The fourth commandment requires us to come to grips with the value of life, with our obligation to nurture it, to care for it, to enable it, to raise it with faith and hope and love.

The second Sinai Tablet is the tablet that challenges us to ethical standards that can make the entire world safe, whole, and fully human. Here we learn that to "love our neighbor as our self" is, indeed, to become a new kind of people, a godly community, a holy nation. Here we learn to protect life, to love unselfishly, to do justice, to build society by honoring truth, to turn our hearts to God rather than to make gods out of the things our heart craves.

To live in the spirit of the Decalogue is to become a healthy, holy, wholesome person.

To live all of the commandments as the Two Great Commandments is to be sure that we are not even tempted to make any one of the commandments themselves the kind of false god that leads us to judge and punish and obstruct a world the purpose of which is to go on in every era growing newly into God.

And then...

I knew a woman once who stayed as far away as she possibly could from minority groups. People challenged her about it but her answer never wavered.

She "wasn't prejudiced," she said. She just didn't understand why they didn't seem to want to "get up in the world." To buy a bigger house. To own a bigger car. She seemed to give no thought that they couldn't get a better job. They couldn't own a house in a better neighborhood. But that was only half the problem.

I think she really did know that there was nothing wrong with these people as individuals. It wasn't their race she feared. It may simply have been that, unadorned and stripped to the essentials, they reminded her of what she herself was inside.

Maybe they reminded her too much of her poverty of soul. Maybe she simply didn't value herself enough as a person ever to come to value the clear and simple personhood of the other.

Maybe she hid herself behind things — the new clothes, the fancy car, the big yard, the elegant house, the things that made her look "respectable," and "successful" — because she was afraid that if others saw her real self, the one without the fancy trinkets and the latest gadgets, they wouldn't like what they saw in her.

We see in others what we fear in ourselves.

That's why the second great commandment is so important. "To love the neighbor as we love ourselves" means that we must also accept in ourselves what there is about us that we don't like, or fear, or devalue.

The second great commandment is a warning to us all; we will reject in others whatever it is that we fear in ourselves.

Only by loving the self to life, by accepting all our own weaknesses, by trusting that the God who loves us will accept the other, too, can we possibly ever really love and accept the other. We might come to tolerate the other, maybe. But we can never really love what we reject in ourselves.

Only self-acceptance with its admission of our own weaknesses, imperfections, mean little smallnesses, and failures can ever truly open our arms to the other.

But we must. Real holiness depends on it. This, Jesus tells us clearly, "is the second — and the greatest — commandment: that we love the other as ourselves."

And for you . . .

When I can admit my own limitations, I can accept the limitations of others. Then I can love them in their struggles, love them in their lack. Then I can stop judging them, berating them, sneering at them. Then I can really love.

All love starts with the way I feel about myself. If I know myself to be sincere, I never doubt anyone else's sincerity. When I know myself to be good-willed, I assume the good will of others. When I know myself to be honest, I trust the other — not to the point of foolishness but always to the point of understanding.

"It is your business," Horace writes, "when the wall next door catches fire." If I realize myself to be responsible for the rest of the world, as well as for myself, I can't possibly say that whatever affects them — legislation, natural disaster, loss of resources — has nothing to do with me.

"It is not by driving away our brothers [and sisters] that we can be alone with God," George MacDonald wrote. In fact, I've often wondered what those people who see no relation between being united with the human race and being united with God take to God to begin with. Narcissism? Just narcissism? So what will they say when God asks them why they were put on earth in the first place?

This commandment asks such embarrassing questions: Do you need medical insurance? Then why wouldn't you do something to get it for everyone else? Do you need to eat? Then why wouldn't you see that every person in the United States is fed? Did you need an education? Then why would you begrudge the tax money it takes to provide a good education for everyone today? See what I mean? Terrible questions.

To intersect with another person's life in any way — as a sales clerk, a doorkeeper, a bus driver, a nurse, a receptionist, a telephone operator, a professional — is to change their lives that day. So the great commandment says to us always, How did you affect someone's life today?

The problem that this commandment presents us with is not "niceness." To be nice is to be safe or political or "genteel." No, the problem with this commandment is that it asks us to be brave and caring and selfishly committed to the care of the other. "You don't have to act as if you care," Richard Dreyfus wrote. "You just have to care enough to act."

William Shakespeare puts it well. He writes: "I do desire we may be better strangers." It isn't that we must all be friends together. It is that we must all be better humans together.

Very little of life, it seems, is fueled by the great commandment. "Saving lives is not a top priority in the halls of power," Myriam Miedzian wrote. "Being compassionate and concerned about human life can cause a man to lose his job. It can cause a woman not to get the job to begin with." It's profit and power, not people, that count. No wonder we think that war is natural.

Once upon a time this commandment made the difference between life and death, between water in the desert or dying of thirst, between starving and gleaning in a neighbor's fields. Now we're in a culture that functions as if people deserve to die if they can't take care of themselves.

If we take time to talk to strangers long enough, more than likely they will say something that confirms the rare idea that they are as human as I am, that they need me, that I know exactly what they're going through. At that moment I finally begin to love them "like myself." But first it takes the talking.

It's that "as myself" stuff in the great commandment where being really moral gets difficult.